Think Straight.
Talk Straight.

First Edition 2019

ISBN: 9780960036509
Library of Congress Control Number: 2018914770

Layout by: AT Impact Consulting, LLC, Dallas, TX
Edited by: Alicia Drury, Rochester, NY

To Carol, Christopher, Jensy, Joshua, and Hannah. Thank you for your unwavering love, encouragement, and support.

To Mom and Dad. Thank you for showing the way.

Contents

ACKNOWLEDGMENTS

This book would not be complete without the support and encouragement of my family—most directly, Carol, Christopher, and Jensy. Joshua and Hannah, your presence and love in my life has served as a significant motivator for me to complete it.

Thank you to my Mom and Dad for who they have been in my life. While I do not remember having deep philosophical discussions with them, or any "Father/Mother knows best" moments, they have simply been good, loving, honest people who helped shape who I am.

I have to thank Rex Houze for the referral to Alicia Drury. Working with Alicia has been a phenomenal experience. She guided me throughout the book writing process, encouraged me when I was frustrated with it, provoked me to look at many things through a different lens, and captured and rewrote many of my thoughts when I struggled with how to express them. I would not have finished it without her assistance and guidance. I would also like to thank Russ Riddle for his periodic legal advice during the book writing process.

My deep appreciation for Arthur Andersen, the founder of the firm at which I worked for over thirty years and reference many times in these pages. While I never knew him personally, his firm shaped me professionally and I am very thankful for that.

Beyond Mr. Andersen, I was touched by many Arthur Andersen people around the globe who represented the values I express in this book. It is not possible to thank them all, but there are several who not only helped me succeed in my career, but became lifelong friends in the process. These include Tim Wille, Bill and Sandie Dillon, Mike Host and Carol Kone, Dave and Linda Ziegler, Jim and Joal Norris, Jim and Debbi Doyle, Bob Philip, and John Miller. Thank you for the professional mentoring I received while at the firm and the friendship and kindness that has ensued.

Thank you to the three executive coaches that I had the opportunity to work with throughout my career: Dr. David Morrison, Dr. Deborah Kiley, and Dr. John "Jack" Jones. Your advice and counsel helped me shape my own executive coaching philosophy. I would also like to thank Jim Blackburn and Tim Kight. I worked with them at different times throughout my career and they helped me form some of my own ideas about leadership and professional and personal growth.

It is impossible to remember and thank everyone who influenced me throughout my business career. There are so many people whose paths have crossed mine and from whom I have benefited in the experience. To all of you—teachers, professors, colleagues, clients, everyone— thank you.

Special Acknowledgment

I wish to acknowledge all of my former colleagues from Arthur Andersen—our alumni. Each of you that I worked with, each of you that I shared a beverage with, each of you that provided me with advice or counsel along the way, had something to do with who I am today. I appreciate you and the impact you had on me. While I occasionally experience the frustration or sadness of knowing the organization no longer exists, I am comforted by the fact that there are thousands of you, all over the world, carrying these messages and affecting positive change in other places.

INTRODUCTION

Throughout my nearly fifty year career in business, I have had the opportunity to meet many people and learn countless things. In the first chapter of my business life, as a partner with Arthur Andersen, I worked on and led many teams. I eventually was in charge of one office, and later of a regional division that included over 1400 employees and partners. I am deeply grateful for those experiences. Beyond accounting and finance, I learned innumerable things about people and business; I had the chance to travel internationally for the first time in my life. I developed a much greater appreciation for the world around me and the variety of people in it. Since retiring from Arthur Andersen and the public accounting profession and beginning my second business life chapter, I have worked with many different people as an executive coach, a mentor, and a volunteer. These individuals have come from even more varied walks of life, businesses, organizations, and backgrounds. They, too, have added immeasurably to my experiences.

In conversations over the years, very often someone would say something like: "Why don't you write these ideas down in a book?" or, "These are good thoughts. They helped me. You should write a book." I would express my thanks for their appreciation and file the thought away. Then in 2010, our first grandchild was born. That set me to thinking.

I don't know very much about my grandfathers. I knew who they were; I knew what they did. But I really didn't know anything about them. Then the accountant in me did the simple math. By the time my two grandchildren (#2 arrived in 2014) are old enough to have a conversation with me about some of the topics in this book, I might not be around or able to engage in a worthwhile conversation with them. If I wanted my grandchildren to know more about me, I needed to do something to make that possible.

For several years, I had been putting some of my thoughts to paper for a newsletter supported by Arthur Andersen alums. So, I started with those and added additional thoughts and observations. The results are what you are about to read.

This book has no particular purpose, other than to share some of my points of view about different facets of business and organizational life, and to share them in a fashion that models the theme of the opening chapter—Think Straight. Talk Straight.® I am not "telling it like it is." I am telling it like I think it is and believe it should be. As I repeat later in the chapter, this is one of the first principles of behavior I learned at Arthur Andersen. It has stayed with me ever since. It is my hope that a few ideas included in this book may resonate with you and my grand-children just like the Think Straight. Talk Straight. principle impacted me all those years ago.

This book is not something you need to read cover to cover, although you certainly can. Look at the topics in the chapter list and select one based on what interests you or fulfills a need at this time. Read it and enjoy it. Each chapter is relatively short, and, I believe, an easy read. A principle I adopted a number of years ago from a Business Writing class told me to "write like I talk." I am not sure I have fully achieved that, but along the way if I have any broken sentences, dangling partici-ples, or faulty punctuation, I hope the spirit of the good sisters of Saint Dominic who taught me grammar school English will forgive me.

I appreciate the many suggestions and encouragement given to me over the years to write my thoughts down. I am thankful for the many rela-tionships with others that have contributed to forming these thoughts. As you read them, I hope they provoke your own thinking and move you to action.

Enjoy!

CHAPTER 1

———

THINK STRAIGHT. TALK STRAIGHT.

Upon retiring from a very successful 34-year career at Arthur Andersen, I stepped out on my own to become a coach. I wanted to use the talents I had developed throughout my career to help others become more effective leaders. In the beginning, I struggled with my own thoughts on coaching leaders. I learned coaching processes from various schools and business training sources, but felt I had to have an overall guiding principle related to my coaching message. After giving it much thought, I kept coming back to the primary tenet I learned from my first day at Arthur Andersen—"Think Straight. Talk Straight."

While I regularly heard this quote, I never read or heard a definition. In a book about the history of the company that carried his name, Arthur Andersen wrote: "About forty-five years ago, my own mother told me in Norwegian, Think Straight. Talk Straight. No finer heritage could possibly be passed on from one generation to another. It has been as a firm rock to which I could anchor in a storm. Never has it failed me . . . This challenge will never fail anyone in a time of trial and temptation."[1] From the time I heard the phrase on my first day of employment with Arthur Andersen, it has never failed me either. It resonates deeply with me in my personal and professional life. In my dealings with others, I lean heavily on the value I find in its meaning.

After further contemplation, I concluded that the words themselves are the definition. But as I began using it in my coaching practice, clients and others would ask me what it meant. So, I defined it for myself and this is how I explain it to others.

Think Straight

Gather the facts. When faced with a problem, assemble the relevant facts to help you think about the problem. Verify those facts as best as possible and in the time allowed. Make your decisions based on the facts, as you understand them. Don't ignore facts that may not support your beliefs. Be prepared to change your belief if the facts warrant.

Understand the context. The same facts may have different meaning in another context. An aspiring college student may have an "outstanding" grade point average, based on the point system in his or her own local high school. It may be equal to the grade point average of another potential college student from a different high school. But, the accepting college may view the two different high schools as having different quality college prep programs and give more credit to the accomplishment of the second student over the first. It is important to remember, context counts.

Avoid noise and fluff. Decisions based on straight thinking are not made in a vacuum. There is always a great deal of "noise" in the system. If it isn't a fact that is relevant to the problem at hand, and if it isn't necessary to understand the context of the situation, then it is unnecessary to consider in the decision making process.

Keep it simple. A number of years ago, one of my clients was the new director of operations in a fairly complex business. He had a strong engineering background and was very knowledgeable of the types of analyses that were necessary for his various managers around the country to use in running their individual company facilities. I had interviewed several of his direct reports, and one of their suggestions was that he simplify some of the reports he used to analyze the business.

When we first worked on this issue, he showed me an incredibly complex spreadsheet that was prepared every month. He used it to monitor the numerous locations and their key statistics and ratios. As a result of our discussion, he redesigned it in such a way that it highlighted problem areas and obvious focal points that required follow-up. He learned that he did not need the same volume and level of data to lead his manager group as he used when he was running an operation himself.

So remember, keep it simple. Even the most complex facts can be broken down into simpler parts. I have always found it helpful to do this to the greatest extent possible. It tends to clear the air and help me focus on what is relevant about the decision or choice I am going to make.

Apply logic to the facts gathered. In my own education, I have learned of two basic forms of reasoning—deductive and inductive.

Deductive reasoning uses deductive arguments to move from given statements or premises to conclusions, which must be true if the premises are true. "All men are mortal. He is a man. Therefore, he is mortal."

Inductive reasoning makes generalizations based on a number of specific individual instances. "Many young drivers receive speeding tickets; therefore, all young drivers drive fast."

Admittedly, flaws can occur in either reasoning, but the point is to apply appropriate reasoning to the facts you have.

Conclude. Once you have the facts you need, understand the context of the problem, filter out the noise and fluff, apply logic to the situation, draw your conclusion from it, and get ready to "Talk Straight."

P.S. It's OK to change your mind. Most of us don't like "flip-floppers." These are people who seem to change their point of view with the changes in the direction of the wind. But this does not mean we should not use the "Think Straight" principles to provoke changing our minds. Many things I believed years ago, which were based on people, organizations and communities I trusted, ultimately proved to be incorrect. They were beliefs that were not fact-based. Am I a flip-flopper because I have changed my mind, in some cases, several times? I think not.

For example, I grew up in an environment that was essentially command-and-control. Our family life, my school years, my military experience, and even a good portion of my work life occurred in a fairly structured environment. Expectations were primarily that to succeed, one did what one was told. In my later years, as I observed organizations continue to be successful, I became less and less enamored with a pure command-and-control leadership structure. Today, as I coach people and watch successful organizations operate, I believe in more of a servant leader-type model. In this environment, leaders focus a good bit of their energy on serving the people they lead, rather than directing everything that those people do. Mind you, even in a servant leader model, there still has to be elements of command-and-control decision making, but it is not the dominant style. Today I am of the opinion that an organization built on integrity and trust—one in which the most junior employee can feel the integrity and trust of the senior leadership and the senior leaders can see that in their junior employees—is the organization that will be successful and stand the test of time. And one more thought that I will repeat often in this book. You must choose the leadership or management style that you believe works best in the specific situation. I am confident you will see that an organization built on trust and integrity can operate effectively whether it is servant leader focused or command-and-control focused.

Well-reasoned changes of the mind over time, as the result of processing experiences and learning, do not mean you are flip-flopping. These changes of the mind further demonstrate you are thinking straight.

Talk Straight

Tell it like it is. Explain the facts to your listener, express the context in which you understand the problem or the issue, and present your conclusion. Don't sugarcoat your answer, but be respectful of the impact your conclusion has on others.

Keep it simple. A number of years ago, in a business writing class, I learned of a concept called the Fog Index.[2] Devised in the early 1950s, American businessman Robert Gunning used the index to assess the complexity in written passages in a document. The result measures the level of difficulty and required grade-level reading skill to sufficiently comprehend the document.

For example, when I "fog" Shakespeare's soliloquy in *Hamlet*, the result is about an "8." Lincoln's Gettysburg address fogs out at about a "9." On the other hand, some of the business documents and government documents I have read easily fog out in the high teens and low twenties.

I believe the principles of Mr. Gunning's Fog Index can also be applied to this principle of talking straight. For example, why say, "Due to extenuating circumstances and significant ramifications precipitated by the unexpected nature and immensity of the current economic downturn, it has become necessary for senior company executives to arrive at the irrefutable conclusion that a reduction in our permanent employee workforce is a forgone conclusion." (Fog Index—over 20)

Instead, you could say, "Business is bad, and we have to reduce our head count." (Fog Index—less than 5)

Effective communication is difficult enough; don't make it more complicated than it needs to be. Be brief and to the point. Add facts and context only as necessary. When too many details are added, it is easier for the point to be lost and comprehension to be compromised.

Ask if you are understood. Inquire if your listener understands what you have told them. If necessary, ask a few questions to validate their understanding. Make sure you agree on what both of you are hearing. Sometimes it is helpful to ask your listener to repeat the message back to you or have them restate the message in their own words.

Consider the other's perspective. It is important to recognize that your listener may not share your point of view. People come to conversations with different viewpoints based on their own organizational, cultural, familial, political, educational, and behavioral backgrounds. You cannot just "Talk Straight" without considering these nuances; but once you do, you should still deliver your message succinctly and directly.

When I was a young partner, I had the opportunity to participate in several meetings with client personnel who came from a different culture. I had spent my entire life up to this point in America and was accompanying a more senior partner of mine who led the discussion. Throughout the meeting, the representatives from the client kept nodding their assent to our comments. After the meeting, I told my senior partner: "Well, that went pretty well! They agreed with everything we recommended!" The senior partner smiled and told me all they had done was acknowledge our comments. Their behavior, which included frequent head nods in the "Yes" direction, were simply to respect our position. They did not include agreement with our conclusions at all. Much to my surprise, he was right. It took several more meetings with the client personnel before we could agree on how to solve the problem.

Be willing to modify your conclusion. If, in the course of the argument or discussion, you obtain new facts or additional context, be willing to build them into your own "Think Straight" process. Change your conclusion, as you deem necessary. Don't be afraid to acknowledge that there might be a different answer. However, do not modify your conclusion if the facts don't support the new point of view, if the context is too muddy, or if the logic is flawed. It is better that the two parties in a discussion respectfully disagree than one agrees for inappropriate reasons.

For example, let's assume you are in a discussion with a customer about a specific deadline for the delivery of a product. Based on your knowledge of the manufacturing and logistics processes within your company, you are absolutely certain that the product can only be delivered within a 25-30 day timeframe from the date of the customer's order. Yet, the customer insists they must have the product within 22 days and threatens to withhold the order if you do not commit. Get a clear representation of all the facts from the customer as to their requirements. Give the customer a clear representation of all the facts about your ability to deliver. If you cannot reduce the gap, all you can do is agree that there is still a three-day difference—and show a willingness to work toward a solution.

Be courteous and respectful. Respect the viewpoint of others. Be thoughtful and polite in listening to others' arguments or presentation. Perhaps explain the context of your conclusion in greater detail, or if available, provide more data in support of your conclusion.

Manage your emotions. Control your emotions and recognize that you cannot control the emotions of others. Think before you speak. In a subsequent chapter, my thoughts on managing your emotions are discussed. Take the time to review it and think about it as you practice the "Talk Straight" principle.

You will benefit from practicing and applying these principles to your communications. One objection I often hear after teaching people to "Talk Straight" is that if you "Tell it like it is" or "Keep it simple," you can sometimes offend someone, hurt their feelings, or de-motivate them. I agree that this can happen if you don't also consider the perspective of others, speak courteously and respectfully, and manage your emotions in the process. But if you combine these techniques, I believe you can "Talk Straight" very effectively, very openly, and with very positive results.

Do I "Think Straight" and "Talk Straight" all the time? No, I do not; but, I try. And, those times when I have not done so have resulted in unpleasantness of some form or another. Do I think that you will "Think Straight. Talk Straight." all the time? I doubt it, but I do hope that it can serve as a guiding principle for you in your life.

I believe in this principle. As I stated earlier, this phrase has served as my guiding principle for most of my professional life. I value it and try to follow it in both my professional and personal life. I hope after reading this chapter and continuing in this book that this principle becomes important to you so that you can benefit from using it in your own way and in your own life. May you be able to think straight and talk straight and discover the benefits of doing so.

CHAPTER 2

SELF-DEVELOPMENT

When was the last time you upgraded your phone or personal computer? Have you recently purchased a new iPad or other form of electronic notebook? What motivated you to upgrade? Was your old model outdated? Slow? Lacking capabilities? As I developed the chapters for this book over the last few years, I have changed my PC, upgraded to the latest version of Microsoft Windows software, and upgraded my iPhone multiple times to the most current model. It struck me that taking steps to keep myself somewhat technologically relevant has almost become second nature to me.

Whether we want to, or just have to, we all fall somewhere on the technology usage spectrum. Some of us have the newest, latest version of whatever gadget or technology tool can help us be more efficient or effective while others of us simply strive to be technologically relevant. But I have a different, and more important question for you. Where are you on the spectrum of developing yourself, and your own skills—not just the tools that can help you practice those skills? When was the last time you looked in the mirror and asked yourself, "Am I the current version of what I need to be in order to be effective, or successful, or whatever I want?" Or, "Am I a 2.0 version in a 4.0 world?"

I frequently ask these questions of clients and others I meet. I am surprised that successful individuals often do not have any particular plan for developing or enhancing their skills. There is no upgrade plan or release date. But why? How can we focus so much time, energy, and money on upgrading technology and so little time and resources on upgrading ourselves? What is standing in our way of self-development?

In his famous book, *The 7 Habits of Highly Effective People*, Steven Covey emphasizes our need to continue to develop ourselves with a habit he titled "Sharpen the Saw." Simply stated by Covey, this means "preserving and enhancing the greatest asset you have—you. It means having a balanced program for self-renewal in four areas of your life: physical, social/emotional, mental, and spiritual."[3]

What have you done recently to "sharpen your saw"? What have you done to renew your physical, emotional, mental, or spiritual self? If you are like most, this question may be more difficult to answer than you may have thought. Often, self-development is not a priority. We allow other things to drain our time and resources so there is little left to invest in ourselves. In other situations, we actually forget that self-development is our responsibility. Instead, we wait and rely on others to develop our skills. We wait for direction, guidance, or a plan of action. We don't wait for someone else to upgrade our technology, so why do we rely on others to upgrade ourselves?

Let me share an example from the first portion of my business career. I worked for Arthur Andersen in the profession of public accountancy. I did not need to concern myself with developing my technical, professional, and behavioral skills. From the day we walked through the door, we were provided with a timetable of the expected growth we would have through the organization. This was accompanied by regular communication about the types of classroom education and training that the firm would provide for us. It was an excellent program to make sure that we were challenged with learning new knowledge related to carrying out our professional responsibilities.

As I matriculated through my career as an auditor, there were four principal professional levels—staff, senior, manager, and partner. One's development path followed these levels:

- The primary focus at the staff level was to execute work steps related to the audit process. The majority of competencies at this level evolved around understanding accounting principles and audit issues and completing audit processes, in accordance with professional standards. The majority of this development was technical in nature.

- At the senior level, we were expected to have an appropriate grasp of the staff competencies and upgrade our knowledge for the more complex technical issues. In addition, we were introduced to the concept of planning and managing an audit engagement, similar to project planning. We learned all aspects of planning a job—logistical, administrative, human resources. Our training at this level continued to include technical competencies for the more complex issues and processes, but we were also introduced to such subjects as job management, time controls, supervising people, building relationships, and client relationship management.

- As managers, our development continued to build and expand on the technical and administrative competencies. Over time we were also expected to develop competencies to manage multiple jobs, deal with a variety of client personnel, expand our industry knowledge, deliver proposals for work, manage budgets, and build long-term relationships with our clients. We were also introduced to the concept of creating relationships for future business opportunities. Our training began to encompass competencies that were more demonstrative of interpersonal skills. These included programs in professional speaking, running meetings, effective business writing, and promoting and selling professional services.

- Those serving as partners continued to be challenged to maintain and develop their competencies in the technical, administrative, and relationship-building areas, but were also expected to have competencies related to broader business skills such as strategy, economics, and global business practices.

My personal plan, which I adjusted each year, aligned with the organization plan, and I greatly benefited from working in an environment that supported individual development. In the early years, most of my development was guided by the firm. As I progressed, I was expected, and sometimes challenged, to build a more personal development plan.

Similar developmental stages exist in many business organizations, whether you are in accounting, finance, engineering, information technology, sales, research, etc. In the early stages of your development, your primary focus is to learn the technical and process skills to support you in your growth. As you grow in the organization and face additional responsibilities, your development needs will broaden into the managerial and leadership categories. You will focus less on the technical requirements of performing your job and more on the relationship and communication skills.

But there are also many organizations and businesses that do not make a significant commitment to the development of their people. They provide their employees with the necessary training they need to use tools that are directly related to the productivity and efficiency of their day-to-day responsibilities. However, training opportunities in areas such as communication, building relationships, emotional intelligence, leadership, basic managerial skills, wellness, etc., are rare.

So, if your organization provides you with regular self-development opportunities, you can probably skim over the rest of this chapter. Be thankful that you work with leadership that invests in the development of their people. But if you are interested in "sharpening your saw" and don't work in an organization that actively promotes you doing so, consider these steps to develop your own personal upgrade plan:

Identify. What do you need to succeed? What competencies are necessary for success in your chosen field? If you are not clear about which skills are important, research the area using available tools. Your organization's human resources department, colleagues, mentors, and your boss can be helpful. Besides learning what is important, you will demonstrate to others that you have a commitment to your own development. While researching what resources are available to you, you may find that your organization has their own personal development and succession planning programs. I am often surprised to find that employees are not familiar with the resources available to them inside their own organization. Seek out these resources and make use of them. If all else fails and you cannot find help inside your organization, head to the Internet.

Consider these questions as you determine what you need:

- What are the future skill additions or enhancements you will need to achieve your personal growth plan?

- Do you have the necessary physical stamina and strength to accomplish your goals? If you do, what will you need to do in the coming years to maintain them? If not, what will you need to do to obtain them?

- Do you have any physical conditions that exist or may be developing that would impair your opportunity to accomplish your goals?

- Have you built or begun to build the appropriate social and professional networks that will be invaluable to you as you strive to achieve your career goals?

- Have you assessed your emotional skills? Are you aware of how your emotions and behaviors positively or negatively affect your ability to continue to grow?

- Do you understand the degree of change occurring in your industry or profession? Have you equipped yourself with the proper tools to help you manage that change and its effect on your future?

- What are the changes happening in your industry or profession that might reduce or eliminate sufficient portions of the knowledge you presently have about that environment? There have been studies that indicate that certain knowledge you obtain today has an expiration date of two years or less. What are your plans to renew yourself regularly?

- As you move through various stages of your own growth, do you have the necessary knowledge to continue to achieve success? Does your plan recognize the changes in responsibilities you will have as you move from associate to a managerial role to a leadership role? Have you factored in the type of development you will need to effectively work in those roles?

- What about your industry? Do you understand the developments occurring in your industry and the rate at which they are changing?

- What are the types of moral or ethical challenges you might face in the future? Are you sufficiently self-aware of your ability to handle those challenges when you are faced with them?

- Is some form or degree of spirituality an important part of your life? If so, how have you accounted for continued development in that area to help you achieve your goals?

These are a mere sampling of the types of development questions you will continue to face as you build your life and your career. The wise person considers these needs as they plan their continued growth.

Evaluate. Once you have identified what you need to succeed, it is now time to evaluate. How are you performing against the expected levels? What competencies do you need to get to the next level? Evaluate your own levels and needs fairly. Large organizations generally have some form of competency identification and performance measurement, often through annual performance reviews. These can provide some insight into your strengths and weaknesses. Use the human resource representatives in your organization to help you identify them. In addition, discuss your thoughts with your colleagues and your boss to get their input. Take advantage of the opportunity to learn from what is already there. Again, if you have had periodic performance reviews, use them as a source for identifying your areas of strength, weakness and potential development. Another source of information about your level of ability, is the people around you—colleagues, your boss, friends, family, etc. Ask them. Throughout your career it is important to be aware of the skills you possess, the degree of competency you have, and the areas in which you need to improve. Every successful individual does this in some fashion. Develop your process and stick with it.

Plan. What steps do you need to take to achieve the appropriate level of competency required in your position? What steps do you need to take to obtain the skills required for the next level of responsibility in your organization? What abilities will you need to achieve your long-term goals? What is your timetable for accomplishing these objectives?

Understand the development program that exists inside your organization. Also, look into professional associations and other organizations that provide learning experiences that might fill your needs. Use all of this information to build your plan for self-development.

Most of us tend to focus more on the present and plan less for the future. We may think about our self-development in terms of skills we need to enhance our productivity or effectiveness in our current employment roles. If you are totally happy and satisfied with your current position, that effort might be sufficient. But it doesn't allow for future growth or changes you wish to make, and it certainly doesn't cover the four areas that Covey says you should sharpen—physical, social/emotional, mental, and spiritual. Remember, self-development is primarily your responsibility. But, self-development should be active, not reactive. Don't wait until it is absolutely necessary to engage in self-development. If you make self-development an ongoing commitment, you will never find yourself in a situation where you are scurrying to perform a much needed personal upgrade.

Once you decide what types of additional learnings you need to achieve your plan, there are plenty of sources to help you plan and navigate your developmental direction. Consider these:

- Business-related developmental areas include technical skills related to your industry and products; managerial skills to run teams, groups, and businesses on a day-to-day basis; and leadership skills to lead people and organizations. For development opportunities in these areas, again I recommend you look to your company and your industry first. Although many businesses have reduced their commitment to expenditures for individual development, you should start there and ask about training programs or other assistance that is available. What types of in-house training programs do they offer? What types of external training or knowledge programs do they offer? What do they pay for, what do they expect their employees to pay for? Research your industry. Are there specific industry programs that exist to help you expand your knowledge? Identify them, evaluate them, and take advantage of them. Consult with your human resources department, your boss, or your mentor.

- Strengthening your physical, emotional, and spiritual well-being may also be supported through your organization's development programs. However, in the case that they are not, there is a wealth of information available to you on the Internet. Do some basic research in these areas. In addition, don't hesitate to consult with members of your community—friends, relatives, etc. Regarding your health and wellness management, talk to your doctor or even your health insurance representatives. More and more, businesses want to help you manage your health. They can offer a variety of ideas to help you focus on preventive maintenance versus repair.

- Use the explosion in information technology as you research and build your development plan. For example, one day I Googled "develop emotional intelligence" and the hits for that alone were over three million. There are plenty of sources available to assist you.

Execute. The final step in my recommended process is the easiest one to explain and often the hardest to do. Work your plan. Adjust it as necessary as requirements change for your organizational responsibilities or expectations, or as your own personal growth goals change. Be relentless in your desire to improve. Use others—colleagues, mentor, direct reports, friends, family—to help you along the way.

This process—identify, evaluate, plan, and execute—is not linear, but continuous. Ask for and listen to feedback as you go through the various stages and make adjustments accordingly.

And as I mentioned previously, if your company has development opportunities through internal sources, that's great. Take advantage of them. But if they don't, don't be dissuaded. Remember, self-development is ultimately your responsibility. There are plenty of good professional organizations and associations, business workshops and local universities to help you continue your development. Do the research and you will find that each of these present a variety of alternatives to your self-development choices—face-to-face workshops, webinars, formal classes, etc.

In discussing this with others over the years, I often hear comments like, "I don't think I should have to pay for this development. After all, the company benefits if I increase my skills." It's difficult to politely tell someone, "Get over it." This process is called self-development for a reason. If your organization is willing to foot the bill for some or all of this training, that is terrific! You work for a great company! But if not, it's still up to you to do it if you want to achieve your personal and business goals. Take responsibility for your own upgrade and remember, more skills and current skills make you more marketable to both your current employer, as well as any future employers.

A final thought about self-development. Think about this: how do you like to learn? When it comes to cognitive learning, each of us has a unique preference. Some prefer visual learning; some prefer auditory learning; some prefer kinesthetic learning. No doubt each of us learns to some extent from each of these styles, but each of us also has a primary preference. If you can learn using your preferred style, both your commitment and comprehension will be higher. Ultimately, your self-development will be more successful.

- Visual learners use objects they can see. They like graphs, pictures and charts. They can also read body language very well and perceive their surroundings well. They are usually good at memorization and recall of information; they have a tendency to remember things that are written down. When they participate in lecture presentations, they learn better by watching the lecturer.

- Auditory learners retain information that they hear and when they speak. They like to be told how to do things and use their listening skills to aid in memorization. They will also often repeat things they hear as an added contributor to their ability to retain the information. While the visual learner reads body language well, the auditory learner notices different aspects of speaking— nuances by the speaker, different volumes and speeds of different speakers, etc. Because of their use of and reliance on auditory skills, they also are people who are talented musically; soft background music may help their concentration.

- Kinesthetic learners prefer to use a hands-on approach to learning. They would rather demonstrate how to do something rather than verbally explain it. They also learn better when they see the learning in action rather than listening to lectures. This type of learner also often prefers working in groups more than the other learners do.[4]

Don't waste your time or resources trying to learn in a way that doesn't work for you. Both your commitment and retention will be higher if you learn using your preferred method.

Have you ever heard the quote, "If you aren't changing, you aren't growing"? I would like to add to that. If you aren't learning, not only are you not growing, you aren't changing. I hope you agree it is important to have your own plan for your life and your career. A significant part of that overall plan should be your plan for continued development of yourself—your plan to sharpen your saw. It is your responsibility. So start sharpening.

CHAPTER 3

———

ACCOUNTABILITY

Whether you read only one chapter or them all, I hope they are helpful to you. It is my intention that they add to your own personal library of information or help reframe your thinking about the various topics discussed throughout this book. In each chapter, I address an issue that I believe often comes to mind for people as they move through their business or organizational lives—strategy, networking, transition, feedback, mentoring, coaching, etc. And in each chapter, I include some ideas for you to consider on how to change your own behavior if, indeed, you feel a change is warranted. However, I only provide the ideas. It is up to you to provide the action. It is your responsibility to hold yourself accountable to put these thoughts to work for yourself. Although accountability is addressed to some extent in other places throughout the book, I thought it fitting to cover it in more depth early on in its own chapter so that you can fully comprehend its importance before reading further.

To get started, let's split the topic of accountability into two separate and unique parts. Often when we hear the word "accountability," what jumps to mind is of holding others accountable. However, what is more important is accountability of self. Holding ourselves accountable for what we commit to do.

In any one of the areas I cover in this book, it is up to you to choose to make a change. If you set a new goal for yourself after completing a chapter, you are agreeing that you will change your behavior. To assure a behavior change, your plan must also include your own accountability mechanism. Your accountability mechanism will help you monitor your goal achievement. At times, your goals will only be modestly achieved or will not be achieved at all because you do not hold yourself accountable. Here are a few thoughts on what you can do to help hold yourself accountable and accomplish your goals:

Enlist others to help. Let's assume your resolution is to accomplish something specifically related to your work environment and the success of your team. Communicate your goal to other members of your team and let them see how it ties into the team's overall goal and to their individual goals. Team members who see that you are trying to align your goal achievement with their success, will most always help your self-accountability. For example, let's assume you are leading a small team of people in a project to design and implement a new technology reporting process within your department. You and your team have developed a detailed plan with appropriate benchmarks, reporting deadlines, and due dates for each team member in their respective roles. As the leader of the team, you also have specific commitments to your boss (or bosses) and to any other peers who might be involved in assisting your team with the development of the project. As a part of your communication with the team, you must help them understand your own deadlines and commitments to others. If you do so, your team members will better understand how their roles and goals fit into the success of the team.

Similarly, if your goal is of a more personal nature, you can share it with a trusted partner. Your trusted partner is someone who willingly holds you accountable; he or she is also someone that you willingly accept feedback from—both positive and negative. And in the best of all worlds, this relationship goes both ways.

Work out an arrangement by which your trusted partner can safely communicate with you about how you are making progress toward your goal. Let me give you an example. An executive coach I knew worked with an executive who had a serious issue. He often lost control of his temper in meetings with his peers. This executive was very committed to the company and to the role of his team in the company's success. But at times, he would be in meetings with his peers—peers whose coordination or cooperation he needed for his team's success. If he sensed that a peer was not coordinating or cooperating, he had a very short fuse and often lost his temper. The coach conducted interviews around this executive. She learned that one of his peers, who was also a supporter and friend of the executive, observed changes in his facial expressions or body language that signaled he was about to lose his temper. The coach arranged a meeting with the peer and the executive. They worked out a signaling system the peer could use to alert the executive when it appeared he was about to lose his cool. Over time, this technique helped the executive accomplish his resolve to control his emotions in difficult situations.

Holding yourself accountable to monitor your own goal achievement does not mean you have to do everything yourself. If you are going to set a weight-loss goal, inform certain key family members or friends of your intentions. Enlist them in helping you with the monitoring process. You will find that most of the people around you want you to be successful in keeping your personal goals. Just like at work, secure the assistance of others to help you monitor goal achievement. Any of those around you in your personal or business life can help by cheerleading your accomplishments and by helping you to get back on track when you slip off the path of accomplishment.

Technology can help. For example, many people who have created self-accountability goals related to improvement of their health have found useful electronic tools in the marketplace (electronic bracelets, smartphone apps, etc.). These devices help monitor progress toward achieving goals. I often use computer software (in my case, Outlook) to help me monitor progress toward keeping my own goals. I can create reminders, prepare notes, and use the alarm system to help me track key items that I want to accomplish. Here is a personal example. Many years ago, I was diagnosed with Type 2 diabetes. Two key aspects of managing this condition relate to periodic testing of my glucose levels and managing my diet. At first, my personal test monitoring relied mostly on my periodic visits to my doctor, even though I had purchased my own self-testing kit. The good doctor gave me some tips on how to remind myself to use the kit more regularly. I did not adopt his ideas as they were not a good fit for me. However, I realized that I referenced my PC calendar (now iPhone calendar) multiple times during the day. So, I put an automatic notification on the calendar to remind me of my daily testing protocols. Over time, it became such a habit that I no longer needed the reminders. My testing device is readily at hand when I need it and it goes with me as a part of my overnight kit on every out-of-town trip. I achieved success by holding myself accountable.

The second step I mentioned above relates to managing my diet. Again, I stumbled a lot in starting to do this. At my doctor's urging, I attended a nutrition class related to diet management for my diabetic condition.

I'll be honest, I did not like what I heard. And it was tough for me to get going on this aspect of my health management. But in brief, I developed my own system for recording my daily food intake. I log my food and details such as calorie and carbohydrate counts. This process has helped me manage my diet much better.

These personal examples may not work for you, but it is up to you to find a method that will. If it doesn't work for you, it will lack staying power and ultimately, fail you. Whatever steps you take, whatever tools you develop and use, you need to have some method of holding yourself accountable in order to achieve your goals.

Be flexible. Another aspect of self-accountability that you should not overlook is flexibility. As you begin to work toward goal achievement, inevitably something will happen that could disrupt your plans. Circumstances change; events occur that might require you to defer them for a short time. Don't panic. Be flexible. Recognize the need to alter your actions. But do something to keep your primary resolve in focus so that you can resume it. If you plan to increase your sales calls by ten per week and you only make seven in the first week, you do not need to up your goal for the following week to thirteen! Your primary focus should be to stay on track toward your original goal of ten per week. Also, remember that you've enlisted others to help. When goal-achievement efforts are disrupted, make sure team members understand what happened and how it will affect the team and them individually. If you notify your team of disruptions on a timely basis, they may even be able to assist you in dealing with the issue and minimize the delay.

Be SMART. I mention this in greater detail elsewhere, but it is important enough to state it here also. Goals you set should be Specific, Measurable, Achievable, Realistic, and Time-framed.

By adapting the four points I just discussed to your own style, you will increase your accountability. You can also use the same four principles when holding others accountable; however, I would recommend two additional points—communication and clarity.

Communication. It is imperative to have regular and ongoing communication with the people you are holding accountable. From day one, communicate with them about their role on the team and the expectations you have for which you will hold them accountable. And you must follow that with periodic communications with them on an ongoing basis to make sure everyone stays on track. For those projects, processes, or work flows that will end, you should have sufficient communication to ensure that they understand the outcomes, how they contributed to the success or what they might have done differently to avoid failure.

Clarity. Communications with team members and between team members require as much clarity as you can muster. Your responsibility as the leader is to make sure that you communicate in a clear and concise manner. In addition, you need to develop a feedback mechanism with your team to know that your communications are being heard loud and clear. Don't assume that just because team members acknowledge that they heard or read your communications that they fully understand what you wish and can execute accordingly. Take appropriate steps within your own communication and leadership style to verify that your communications are being received and acted upon appropriately. If you do this regularly, you will find that you will have to do less validation or verification over time. Trust will build, the team members will develop their own skill of self-accountability and your job of holding them accountable will be much easier.

As with most behaviors, it is important to remember that others will be watching you and taking notice of your personal accountability. Do you hold yourself accountable? Do you follow through with your accountability of others? As a leader, it is your responsibility to set the standard for accountability within your team, group, or department. Let them see how you hold yourself accountable. Follow through on your accountability of others so they know what to expect and they will strive to meet your expectations. Employees that feel accountable for their actions will work harder to achieve the goals of the company, ultimately improving company success. And employees that see you hold yourself accountable will help you do the same with them.

Like all other behaviors and skills discussed in this book, self-accountability and accountability of others improves over time as it is practiced. So, get out and practice, practice, practice.

CHAPTER 4

——

COACHING

Throughout my life, I have interacted with many coaches for multiple different reasons. In fact, it is probably safe to say that nearly everyone reading this book has utilized a coach at some point in their life. But for what reason?

Some individuals have probably used a coach for a sport. Soccer. Baseball. Volleyball. Tennis. Swimming. You name it. But how many of us have used a career coach? A life coach? An executive coach? Has it ever occurred to you to employ a coach of this type?

The Olympics is one of the most significant sporting events in the world. Thousands of athletes come from across the globe to compete in their individual sport. Do you think an Olympic athlete would compete without the help of a coach? I doubt it. In fact, I can't conceive of anyone attempting to perform at the level of an Olympian without the benefits of a coach. Can you?

As you may know by now, I am an executive coach. Coaching others is not only my passion, it is my purpose. When people ask me why they should make use of a coach in their business or personal life, I answer them with two names—Tiger Woods. Michael Phelps. In my lifetime, I have had the good fortune to see these two athletes compete numerous times in their individual sports. Clearly, these two world-class athletes have not achieved their success alone. Throughout their storied careers, they have had coaches to help them. They understand that an elemental resource to attaining their desired level of success is a coach.

In the time that I have watched Tiger Woods, he has engaged at least three coaches to help him with his swing. In an interview I saw with

Michael Phelps, Michael acknowledged that after his success in the Beijing Olympics, he did not commit himself as hard to his training. When he recommitted for the London Olympics, he immediately looked to his longtime swim coach to help him prepare. If these two superior athletes, who are clearly at the top of their game, recognize the need to work with a coach, why don't we? Why do so many of us dismiss the possibility of using a coach to help us get through some of our own challenges in work or life? Why don't we think about using a coach to help us "reengineer our swing"—to help us strengthen a behavioral area that can improve our performance? Remember what I said about being a 2.0 version in a 4.0 world?

We all have an idea about what a coach is. But take a moment to really think about it. My favorite Internet research source, Wikipedia, says that the word coach is derived from the name for the village of Kocs in Hungary.[5] Kocs is credited as being the birthplace of the horse-drawn carriage around the fifteenth century. So a "kocs" (coach) was used to help people get around. Many years later, the word evolved on college campuses for tutor. Speculation is that this arose because tutors were thought to "carry" students through to their examinations. Over time, the term came to be used to describe "athletic teachers" also. Whether these are correct suppositions or not, the term coach evolved to be what it is today—someone who instructs or trains another.[6]

The primary job of a coach is to help you work on certain skills or behaviors that you wish to improve. For example, consider a professional golfer. She has been playing well, but all of a sudden she has trouble making a certain type of shot. No matter what she tries to do, she cannot execute the shot in the desired manner or with the success she had in the past. Consequently, she engages a coach to work with her. Together, they identify the nuances that are necessary to alter her swing. The coach helps her assess the current state of her swing, develop a plan to adjust the swing, practice the new swing behavior, use the new swing in appropriate tournament situations, and measure her results. She takes these new ideas, or in some cases, is reminded of ideas from the past, applies them, and successfully achieves her goal of shaping and making that shot. If her shot results improve, she will adopt these new behaviors as a part of her swing pattern for that shot. If not, then it is back to the coach to work on other solutions.

Now, let's shift our focus to the business world, where unfortunately, coaches are underutilized. Let's say a business person takes on a new leadership role. Within a short period, turnover in his department spikes. Instead of trying to fix the problem alone, the new leader decides to engage a coach to help him analyze the impact of his leadership style on those around him. Working with the coach, he will assess the current state of behaviors, identify what might need to be altered, develop a plan to implement new behaviors, execute against that plan by changing behaviors, and measure the results of the changing behaviors. Just as with the golfer, if the outcome is positive and departmental turnover is reduced, he continues the new behaviors. If not, he continues to search for the solution.

A few years ago, I worked with an aspiring executive who was at the manager level in a large company. He was in this role for a couple of years and was performing well as a project manager. He made significant contributions to the success of his team, and had good relations with his boss, his direct reports, and his peers. His projects were always delivered on time; he met his target deadlines and commitments regularly. His boss felt he could be relied on to lead any project successfully.

His boss considered him to be a very reliable and dependable manager who would complete his projects on time and within budget. He regularly communicated with his boss and kept him informed of any glitches that arose.

When I became his coach and interviewed his boss about his performance and work behaviors, I learned that the boss' expectations were not being fully met. The boss did not just want him to accept new responsibilities and do them well. The boss expected him to be proactive and seek out new responsibilities. The manager was not showing that initiative.

In one example, the boss said he told his team they had to prepare a significant presentation for senior leadership about a new product under development. To complete the project, a leader had to assemble a significant amount of research information that the team had been working on, analyze the data, and prepare an executive level presentation. He wanted this manager to lead the group in the development of the presentation. However ,when he told his team about the project, two of the other direct reports immediately volunteered to help, whereas this manager did not. The boss was disappointed because this company valued those employees who effectively used their technical skills, but who also showed leadership potential by volunteering to take the lead on new projects or initiatives. They had to be willing to self-promote. This manager did not display that willingness.

Along with interviewing the boss, I spoke to several of this manager's peers and his direct reports regarding his leadership skills. While most feedback was positive, one issue repeatedly arose. His team knew that their manager was very knowledgeable when it came to the subject of research and development, and they enjoyed working with him on different project teams. But again, they did not feel that he spoke up sufficiently to upper management about the team's accomplishments or new ideas they developed.

Since the manager was working to improve his leadership skills, he and I discussed this behavior in one of our coaching sessions. He explained his perspective on his behavior. We agreed that this was an area in which he could comfortably change his behavior. We talked about upcoming work opportunities in which he could practice his new skills, and set appropriate goals. At subsequent meetings, we reviewed our progress.

By the time we completed our formal coaching project together, he was bringing fresh ideas to the table. In addition, he had volunteered to take the lead on some projects his boss wanted to accomplish. This also increased his visibility with his direct reports, his peers and his boss and their recognition of his leadership skills and potential.

Throughout both my personal and professional life, I have had the opportunity to meet many coaches in various lines of work. Most coaches have similar processes they follow to help people change or alter specific behaviors. A coach will help you:

- Identify ineffective behaviors.

- Determine actionable items to change the behavior(s).

- Work with you to help you make the change.

- Help you evaluate improvement.

A simple yet effective coaching process I use in my practice is:

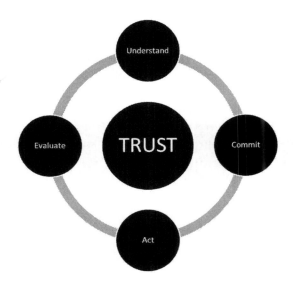

Understand. In this phase, I conduct interviews to learn more about the individual—background, behaviors, and business. This may include interviews with the individual along with their direct reports, peers, boss, customers, or vendors. I may also assess existing behaviors and potential for growth with various assessment tools.

Commit. In this phase, the individual commits to building their skills as a leader. We work together to identify a plan to do so.

Act. Once commitment has been made, the individual begins to practice the different skills and continues to strengthen the behaviors that have made them successful.

Evaluate. In this phase, we measure growth and build on the foundation that has been established to continue future growth.

Trust. Naturally, all of this activity has to take place in an environment of trust. I must be trusted as the coach and I must trust the person being coached.

This is an iterative process. By this, I mean that we may begin the step of acting on the development plan, but then decide that a different behavior needs to be changed. If agreed, you return to the commitment stage of the process, agree on the change that will be made and then proceed.

Each coach or coaching company has their own process. If you are engaging a coach, you should understand their process first and make sure you are comfortable with it before you begin your journey together. No change will take place if there is a lack of commitment.

Another aspect of coaching individuals relates to the concept of life coaching. In my practice as an executive coach, I focus on people in business and other organizational settings. My goal is to help them be more efficient, productive, organized, or strategic. We work together to help them improve their leadership skills or competencies. While this occasionally tips over into dealing with personal or interpersonal relationship issues, I do not focus on life coaching. However, there are coaches who do so. Often, individuals will engage a life coach to help them with such issues as managing their work/life balance more effectively, developing a plan for achieving life goals beyond the work environment, etc.

If you decide that you wish to engage an executive coach or a life coach, here are some steps that I suggest you follow:

- Make a list of the competencies or skills that you would like to strengthen or improve.

- Research the sources for coaches in your area. If there is a Human Resources department in your company, ask if they have coaching resources they recommend or what the process would be to engage one. If there is no internal source available to help find a coach, a good place to start is with the International Coach Federation (ICF) website (www.coachfederation.org). In addition to describing the benefits of working with a coach, the ICF website can be used to obtain referrals to appropriate coaches in your community. You can contact one of the local ICF chapters and identify resources through them. Also check with friends, relatives, or colleagues to identify others who have worked with a coach.

- After you identify the resources in your area, contact a few of them and interview them to see if they will be a good fit for you. Consider their background, apparent coaching style, and individual coaching process—contemplate how you feel about working with them on a personal level. You should feel comfortable enough to discuss almost anything with them in a coaching session. Many coaches will offer an initial session at no cost to you. This test drive should give you a good sense of whether or not you will want to work with him or her.

- Make your selection and begin the process.

Whether you are striving to achieve a specific promotion in your organization, to lead a team on a specific project to a defined solution, or to run the best department or division in your company, we can all benefit from using a coach at certain times.

Remember, the primary job of a coach is to help you work on certain skills or behaviors that you wish to improve. So, if you have a behavior you want to change, and you find it challenging to address on your own, hire a coach to help. A coach won't change your behavior, but a coach will help you build the courage you need to make a change. Once you are armed with both knowledge and courage you will be able to implement the changes you would like to see and become a better performer as a result.

CHAPTER 5

MENTORING

It would be easy to assume that coaching and mentoring are the same thing. So much so that in the business environment, the terms are often used interchangeably. In reality, the two roles differ greatly. It is possible that in your career, you may find yourself in both of these essential roles.

Have you ever asked yourself, "Should I have a mentor?" Or have you ever found yourself wondering, "Should I be a mentor?" Have you been asked by another, "Would you mentor me?" Often, these questions are immediately followed up by related questions such as, "What is mentoring? What does a mentor do? How is mentoring different from coaching?"

Throughout my coaching career, I have been asked numerous times, "If someone asks me to be a mentor, should I accept the responsibility and become one?" I have also frequently been asked, "Do I need a mentor?" Like so many other questions, the answer is "It depends."

First, let me clarify what I mean by a mentor. Again, according to my favorite research source, Wikipedia, the word *mentor* was derived from Homer's "Odyssey." Mentor was Odysseus' loyal friend. When Odysseus ventured off to fight the Trojan War, he gave Mentor the responsibility of nurturing Telemachus (Odysseus' son).[7] In this context, a mentor is a trusted guide and counselor. When implemented correctly, the mentor-protégé relationship is a deep and meaningful association and one that comes with responsibility—for both parties.

Coach vs. Mentor

Although there may be some overlap, a mentor is not a coach. As stated in the previous chapter, a coach will help you work on certain skills or behaviors that you wish to improve. A coach helps you change a behavior to achieve a specific result—something to improve your immediate performance, as in our earlier example of the golf swing.

A mentor, however, is quite different. Whereas a coach will focus on skills or behaviors, a mentor will help you understand and navigate your environment. A mentor, generally, does not focus on skills and behaviors.

After a while, the roles of the coach and the mentor may blend. Typically, the coach's role ends when the particular behavior change is achieved. The mentor's role, however, may extend much longer and may even extend beyond the current workplace.

Let's go back to the golfer example I gave you in the previous chapter. A coach will help the golfer work on her swing in order to improve her game. A mentor, on the other hand will help her consider matters such as the tournaments in which she should play, the types of business or professional affiliations to consider in order to promote her career to the public, and how best to develop her career path from amateur to professional.

In business, a mentor may help an aspiring executive consider which career path might be best for her, determine what learning activities she should consider to enhance her professional growth, define the intermediate career steps she should take to achieve a long-term career objective, or learn and navigate the culture of a new organization she has just joined.

So if a mentor is not a coach and a coach is not a mentor, what is mentoring and why should you consider it? Before we discuss the mentor/mentee relationship, let's start by looking more closely at mentoring.

What is mentoring?
Contrary to what many may believe, mentoring is not "on the job training." We don't mentor people to offer them corrective or remedial instruction. It is also not casual water cooler or over the counter advice. Mentoring is not one-size-fits-all. Nor is it necessary that everyone always have a mentor. Mentoring is not the relationship between boss and direct report; in fact, I do not believe your mentor should be your

boss. It is my opinion that a mentor should be someone senior to you who knows you as well as the organization or business in which you work. It may be another person senior to you in the company. It may be someone more experienced than you from outside the company.

The relationship between the mentor and mentee is often misunderstood. Simply stated, mentoring is a *partnership* between the mentor and the mentee where both parties will benefit from the relationship. It is a relationship built on *trust* that provides value to both participants. It helps you identify steps to enhance both your career and life. The mentoring relationship gives the mentee and the mentor an opportunity to grow and develop *each other* through a business relationship. It commits both parties to each other's learning and development. It is a relationship that maintains confidence, builds trust, and challenges each other's thinking.

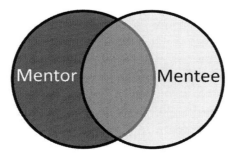

In a mentoring relationship, the mentee must work in partnership with the mentor to build trust and respect confidentiality. As you get to know each other, you will be more comfortable sharing information. As you communicate, you must strive to be open and honest—to think straight and talk straight. This also means that there must be an understanding by both individuals that conversations are confidential. This aspect of the relationship is especially important if the mentor and mentee work within the same company. If you are a mentor, it is absolutely critical that your mentee know that he can share anything with you and it will not go beyond your mutual conversation, and vice versa.

The mentee should be encouraged to share her goals and dreams. The mentor should not second-guess them, but should challenge the mentee if the mentor observes that current behaviors are inconsistent with the goals being discussed. The mentor should also help the mentee evaluate whether or not the goals are realistic.

For example, let's assume that you are a chemical engineer who has been out of college for a few years. You have an undergraduate degree in chemical engineering and you have been pleased with your assignments in the company you joined. You are in the research and development division of a global pharmaceutical company. You are on track for continued growth and development. A senior executive in your division has been mentoring you since you joined the company, and you trust and appreciate her interest in your career. You recently met with her and discussed your goal to become a Director of Research in the division. You would like to achieve that in three years. However, as you have observed, all of the Directors in your division had twelve to fifteen years' experience with the company before they were promoted to Director. In your conversation, she informed you that the company's policy is to have each associate work in different areas of the company's research division before they can be promoted to Director. She strongly recommended that you consider this and redirect your short-term goals to obtain experience in two or three other areas within the division before you focus on a Director promotion. She even had some recommendations on the order you should follow as you take on these different responsibilities. Her point of view is that if you demonstrate a consistent skill level across the division, your opportunity to be a Director will significantly improve. You may not like this answer, but she has done her job as a good mentor to explain this approach to you. If, however, you disagree and still want to try for an earlier promotion, she will continue to be a good mentor if she reminds you of the difficulty, but also helps you devise a plan that might help you achieve your goal.

The importance of listening

Good listening skills are imperative to the success of a mentoring relationship. In John Maxwell's book, *Winning with People*, he states, "People don't care how much you know until they know how much you care."[8] Like John Maxwell, I believe the most important thing you can do to demonstrate that you care is to be a great listener. Do this and you will be a great mentor.

For a mentee to be a good listener, it does not mean to accept on faith everything the mentor says. If you have concerns or issues with the points being raised, you should challenge your mentor and discuss them. The same is true for the mentor. The mentor should listen carefully to the mentee describe his issues and concerns, but not be afraid to challenge the facts or assumptions on which they are based. But remember, as a mentor you should listen carefully and challenge politely, not question ruthlessly or interrogate.

In any mentoring relationship, both the mentee and mentor should be willing to learn together, grow together, and continue their personal and professional development. Depending on the situation, the mentor can suggest learning opportunities, training programs, classes, books, etc., that can be beneficial to the mentee. Similarly, the mentee should feel that she can suggest ideas for continued development to the mentor.

As a senior businessman, I have worked in mentoring programs for undergraduate college students as well as for young professionals and managers. Based on feedback I have received, I know I have helped my mentees learn, grow, and develop. But I also know that I have grown and developed as a result of my relationship with them. In this regard, I have one bit of advice for senior mentors: you have to let your mentee know that you want them to share ideas they have about your development, just as you share yours with them. It can be something as simple as suggesting a new iPhone application or a website to visit. You build your trusted relationship with your mentee when you do so.

Feedback

Both parties in the mentoring relationship should be willing and feel encouraged to give feedback to each other. An easy way to practice this is to make sure that every meeting ends with a brief conversation on what each of you got out of the interaction. A colleague of mine has a great "end of meeting" habit. After each meeting she asks, "What did you get out of today's meeting? What is your takeaway?" That can be a simple way to close each mentoring conversation. Further, since it is the role of the mentor to lead in the relationship, she can start by sharing her thoughts on what she got out of the conversation. In a later chapter on feedback, we also discuss Marshall Goldsmith's idea of "feedforward." You and your mentor can also practice this technique in your discussions.

Scheduling

The mentee should take the primary responsibility to schedule appointments and send out reminders. This action demonstrates how committed the mentee is to having a mentoring relationship. Some mentors and mentees like to schedule regular meetings or phone conversations. Find out what works best for each of you and come to an agreeable solution.

Once an appointment is scheduled, be sure to plan accordingly. Show up on time for the appointment, promptly start the meeting and deliver any promised results in accordance with an agreed upon schedule. Your timeliness shows that you respect the other individual and the commitments he has.

In today's environment, it is also helpful to decide how you will communicate the basic things like appointments, reminders, etc. Some people prefer email; others, voicemail; others, texting. Agree about communication preferences early in the mentoring relationship and do what works best for both parties.

Commitments

Both individuals must follow through on commitments. If the mentor promises to send the title of a recent book they read, they should make a follow-up note to do so. It should also be agreed that each party will hold the other accountable. In this case, if the mentor forgets to send the book title, the mentee should not feel intimidated to remind them. As the relationship grows, mentors and mentees will learn what accountability techniques work and when it is necessary to ask permission to employ a technique.

Be careful to not over commit. Find a schedule that works for both parties involved. If the schedule doesn't work, it won't last. So work together to decide what will work best to maintain a high level of commitment. If the agreed upon schedule is not working, don't be afraid to change it. The relationship will only work if both parties are committed to its success.

Other tips

Here are a few other tips to help strengthen your mentoring relationship:

- Share stories and experiences. After all, experience is the best teacher. Don't be afraid to tell "war stories." You may think they are boring, but I guarantee you that most mentees will not. After you share a story, share the lesson you learned with your mentee. He will appreciate you doing so. And, the stories don't always have to be successes. Let's face it: some of the best learning experiences we have had came from mistakes or failures. Also, stories can be contributed by the mentee; they don't just come from the mentor. I have often benefited from one of the stories that a mentee shares with me. You can find more information on storytelling in Chapter 22.

- Model the appropriate behavior. You can do serious damage to a mentoring relationship if your mentee sees you behaving unprofessionally or in a manner that is inconsistent with your own advice. Even if you don't work in the same area in the organization, trust me, any bad behavior on your part will filter back to your mentee. You must "walk the talk." As a mentor you wear many hats—sponsor, teacher, guide, counselor, protector— know when to behave like each. Be consistent in that behavior.

- Enjoy your mentoring relationship; have fun in it. The conversations don't always have to be heavy and serious. They can be lighthearted and humorous. Activities you might share together don't always have to be job-focused; they can also be social events.

As you think about having a mentoring relationship with another, you may wonder how often you should meet as mentor and mentee. You might also wonder how long this relationship should last. As I said in the opening of this chapter—it depends. If you are participating in a formal mentoring program, there might be some specific, outlined requirements to have conversations between the mentor and mentee on a regular, periodic basis—for example, once a month. If it is a relationship that is not structured through a formal mentoring program, then the mentor and mentee should agree on an approximate schedule of participation, test that pattern for a while, and adjust it as necessary. Most of my mentoring activities have occurred on an approximate monthly basis. Length of time is also very flexible. Formal mentoring programs often are designed to work for a year at a time. It is up to the mentor and mentee how long they want to carry it on. I had one mentor that I met with for several years. Some years, we scheduled regular appointments. In others, it was more random and depended on my need for his advice. Like water, these relationships tend to find their own level.

Getting started

In other chapters, I will explain that in order to be successful in life or business, you have to understand how your behavior is seen by others. It helps to pay attention to how the behavior of others is different from yours. This is also an important concept in a mentoring relationship. I don't think two parties in a mentoring relationship need to complete a full behavioral assessment, but it is important to understand something about how each other behaves. As you begin your mentor-mentee relationship, share with each other your thoughts about what you like and don't like about different behaviors in the workplace and life. Continue to discuss these differences as your mentoring relationship evolves. Behavior styles can be complex and affect the way you both approach a problem-solution situation. For example, some people prefer extensive data analysis to help determine a solution while others focus on the people impact of the solution. Or they can be simple communication style differences: "If you need to call me, don't call me during normal business hours unless it is a crisis." Or, "I don't respond quickly to phone calls, but I will respond quickly to text messages." Refer to my discussion on behavior assessments in Chapter 14 for more discussion on this topic. Don't overlook the importance of understanding each other's behavior styles. If you can understand the differences in behavior styles, you can accomplish a lot more in your communication. Understanding your own behavior helps you understand the behavior of others. It enhances your ability to communicate and to manage your emotions in relationships. Spend a little time on it in your mentoring dialogue. As you work together for success, be willing to share observations about behavior style along the way. Investing time early on in your relationship to understand styles will pay off later on and will ultimately save time in the end due to a stronger knowledge of each other.

If you are feeling like Telemachus and don't have a Mentor and would like to work with one, consider the following steps:

- Check with your organization's Human Resources department and find out if a formal program exists; if it does, ask if you can participate. If it does not, discuss with them about how you should approach finding a mentor in your company or even within your industry.

- If a formal program does not exist, ask yourself, "Which senior person in my organization do I think would be a good mentor for me?" Then go ahead and ask them!

- If you would prefer a mentor from outside the organization, identify an appropriate person and approach them with a similar request.

- Develop your own goals and objectives and prepare to discuss them with your mentor.

- Agree on and arrange logistics about where to meet, frequency, etc.

- Get to know each other and begin the process.

- And remember, have fun!

If you have never been involved in a mentor-mentee relationship, I strongly encourage you to give it a try. It is truly a rewarding experience. Whether you are Telemachus or Mentor, I have no doubt you will grow and benefit from the relationship. You will build a relationship with someone new and will have an impact on the development of the other person in the relationship. Throughout your journey, you will even learn some things about yourself and be better prepared to navigate your future.

Coaching and mentoring

I hope these last two chapters help you understand the differences between coaching and mentoring. Sometimes the differences are quite clear; often times they are more subtle and may even overlap. You will find that as a coach, you sometimes are acting more like a mentor; and sometimes as a mentor, you are acting more like a coach. Mentoring ideas described in this chapter are often used in coaching, and vice versa. The importance of each is that they are useful relationships that help others develop as well as yourself.

CHAPTER 6

———

LISTENING

Throughout the last two chapters you have read several times about the importance of listening. While most of us recognize its importance in everyday life, we may lack the skills necessary to be a successful listener. If I asked you to rate your listening skills on a scale of one (lowest) to ten (highest), how would you score yourself? Do you consider yourself a good listener? Are you an average listener or a poor listener?

Would you agree that poor listening is costly? Misunderstandings resulting from poor listening can cost us valuable time. Poor listening can hinder relationships by causing the other person to feel unimportant, or worse. Poor listening can lead to arguments and conflict. It can lead to misapplication of procedures or processes that can cause irreparable harm. In fact, I can't think of anything positive that results from poor listening, can you? Well, actually, I can. The one positive thing about poor listening is that you can change it. You *can* become a better listener.

In another chapter, I discuss storytelling and how to tell a good story. You know, the one everyone wants to listen to. The story that is so good that others want their chance to re-tell it. Isn't it true that listening is easy when we are really engaged in what is being said? We are captivated, interested, and eager for more. But what happens to our listening skills when the speaker isn't captivating? When the topic is not of interest to us, or the delivery is falling flat? Does our ability to listen change?

I learned a valuable lesson about listening from my young grandson. One Christmas Day when he was about four years old, I observed him opening his presents. As he quickly dismantled the delicate wrapping efforts of his parents, grandparents, aunts, and uncles, I noted something interesting about his listening skills.

When a new gift was unexciting or mundane in his mind, he was eager to place it aside and move on to the next present. He would respond to adult questions about whether or not he enjoyed the gift—even though it might have been a pair of socks or pajamas—with a quick "yes." That appeared to be the automatic default answer for a gift that had little or no value to him.

Then there were the gifts that were intriguing to him—the toy or game he did not know its purpose. With those he was inquisitive. He asked what it was, what it was for, and listened during the explanation. He paid attention to what was being said.

The third category of gifts were the ones he found exciting. He immediately knew what it was—often what movie or TV character it represented. He studied it eagerly and when asked direct questions about it, the questioner was met with resounding silence. It was the "don't bother me" mode; it reflected his lack of interest in what you wanted because he was totally wrapped up in his own world. Interestingly, this is also often his listening mode when an adult is in his territory and tells or asks him to change a behavior. Although you are less than five feet from him, and he has the average hearing of any active young child, it's like he is on another planet. It doesn't surprise me that he is developing listening skills at his age that are very frequently demonstrated by the adults around him. My lovely wife calls it "selective listening" when I employ it in my own conversation.

Think about how similar these Christmas morning scenarios are to our everyday lives and our ability to listen. Let's analyze this a little more.

- How often in a business or personal mode do you quickly, yet unintentionally respond to the question of another, either by cutting them off in half-sentence or responding sharply in a way that says, "I am not really interested in your question. Let's move on to the next item of importance to me?"

- How frequently do you get so wrapped up in your own thinking or activities that communications from others seem to fall on deaf ears? Whether you hear the question or not, how often do you act like you are not hearing the other person and continue to do what you are doing?

- How often do you respond directly to the comment or question of another person by showing you are interested in what they are saying or asking?

- How frequently do you enter into a dialogue that demonstrates you are listening to their point of view and are genuinely interested in what they are saying?

Listening skills are, in many cases, second nature. They are habits. The way you respond to others in a listening situation is often unintentional. So if you feel you need to address a weakness in your listening skills, it is no different than changing any other habit. For some period of time, you will have to work on the skill specifically. As you prepare for key conversations, you will have to think about how you are going to be listening. You have to be intentional about using the new skill until you have used it so much, you are using it unintentionally and have formed a new habit. Also, there are going to be some situations, with some people that you always have to consciously and intentionally focus your listening skills.

Fortunately for all of us, listening is a skill that we can continue to develop over time. Regardless of how well you rated your listening skills in the beginning of this chapter, there is always room for improvement. So I challenge you to become a better listener, and a more active listener by employing some of these tips.

Be aware of your body language. Does your seated or standing posture tell the other person that you are actively engaged in the conversation? Or, do you slouch in your seat or slump in your stance and telegraph to the other that their words are not all that important to you?

Very recently, I interviewed an executive about a very specific topic. In this case, she had some very strong points of view related to the matter at hand. I feel confident that I asked good questions and showed interest in her responses. However, after the interview I was given feedback that the executive felt as though I did not really seem interested in her point of view—that I had already made up my mind about the resolution of the topic at hand and that I was just paying lip service to her position on the matter. Nothing could have been further from the truth. However, when I thought about some of the things I did during the interview, I realized that my posture and body language could have created that impression even if my words did not.

Maintain good eye contact. Where are your eyes during a conversation? Are you focused on the person who is speaking with you or are you looking around the room, or sweeping the floor for foreign particles? Even if you are looking at the person, are you looking at their feet, or their hands rather than looking them in the eye? This one hit home to me a number of years ago. I was a young partner in our firm, and I attended a networking reception with a number of my partners from around the firm, many whom I had not met. Several were in significant leadership roles within the organization. I wanted to make sure I had the opportunity to speak individually with each of them. In all honesty, I was probably a little too eager to try to show myself off. I happened to be in a conversation with one of the other partners in my office. He was not my immediate boss, but in the hierarchy, he was slightly ahead of me in rank. Just after we broke off our conversation to mingle with some of the others, he took me aside and said, "Ed, if you ever talk with me again and I see that your eyes are roaming around the room, I will end our conversation abruptly and we won't have many more in the future." Needless to say, I was taken aback by what he said. But in being honest with myself, I also recognized that he was right. Since that time, I have redoubled my efforts to give appropriate attention to the person with whom I am speaking.

Practice good nonverbal habits. Non-verbals can also tip off your lack of listening. Along with your body language and eye movement, recognize that there are other nonverbal habits that indicate whether you are really listening. These include facial expressions, hand and arm gestures, squirming around in your chair, tone of voice, and how fast or slow you are speaking. You also frustrate the other person when you interrupt them in mid-sentence, or jump ahead and end their sentences for them. It is important to exercise self-control both verbally and non-verbally when engaged in conversation. Even if you know what the other person is going to say, be quiet and let them say it. You can always add your own thoughts after they conclude theirs.

Remember, non-verbals are also a two-way street, so pay attention to those exhibited by the person with whom you are speaking. You can learn a lot from what another person is conveying to you non-verbally. Some nonverbal cues suggest discomfort with the topic being discussed and require more probing questions on your part. Others indicate the time for the conversation is over. Others will show that the person to whom you are listening feels that you are grasping the essence of their comments.

Repeat, reflect, or reframe. By repeating or reflecting on the statements made by the other person, you show them that you are attentively listening to their points. For example, assume the other person says, "We cannot seem to get a handle on the drop in production we have had in our Cuyahoga plant in the last two months." You might say, "As I understand it, over the past couple of months you have had a drop in production in Cuyahoga. You have tried to analyze the drop, but so far you have been unsuccessful in determining the cause." Or the other person might say, "We are pretty pleased with our sales increase in the past month – it was up over 11%." And you say, "Yes, our initial analysis pegged your increase at 11.3%." When you reframe, you simply help the person see the problem from another perspective. For example, in a coaching situation a person might say, "My boss says I am too much of a stickler for details. I get hung up on details too often. I have to stop doing that." The coach might reframe the issue by asking, "What are some situations in which you recall that your attention to detail was beneficial to you—and to your boss?" These are great techniques to help you clarify what the other person is saying and help them focus on the issue at hand, while also demonstrating that you are listening attentively.

Minimize distraction and interruptions. Distractions and interruptions can also affect our listening ability. As much as we all would like to believe that we are good multitaskers, neurologists and other brain scientists insist that the human brain, although it operates at nano-speeds, does not multitask. It is impossible to be fully engaged in a conversation if you are also typing a document, surfing the Web, or texting.

While conducting a recent telephone interview, I could hear constant clacking in the background. It sounded like the person on the other end was working at a keyboard at the same time of the interview. I not-so-subtly mentioned that I heard a clacking noise in the background and that there might be some interference on the phone. I asked whether I should switch from my cell phone to a land line. The person I was speaking to somewhat sheepishly acknowledged that when he picked up my call he was finishing an important report that he had to get to his boss. He just needed a few more minutes to do so. I responded, "No problem. I will call you back in ten minutes so that you can concentrate 100% on your report and your attention is not deflected by my questions." He appreciated my concern for his situation and ten minutes later I had his full attention and we had a very good conversation. Sometimes it will be beneficial to pause a conversation until a time when both parties can be fully engaged. If you think this is the case, tell the other party you are going to defer the conversation until you can give it your full attention. This will help ensure the intended message is fully understood by both parties.

Seek to understand. Understanding is yet another skill to practice when improving your listening skills. In his landmark book, *The 7 Habits of Highly Effective People*, Stephen Covey's fifth habit is "Seek first to understand, then to be understood."[9] This is great to keep in mind when exercising your listening skills. Your primary role as a good listener is to understand the facts presented by the other party, the assumptions that they have made in drawing their conclusions about those facts, and the emotions or feelings they have about the issues emanating from those fact and emotions.

Ask good questions. One of the most effective ways to gain understanding is to ask good questions. Questioning is an excellent listening skill. It's simple. Ask the right kind of questions during a conversation, and you stimulate the thinking of the other party. Your questions help them generate additional thoughts to clarify their communication.

I am sure you know the difference between open-ended and closed-ended questions. Often our communications training encourages us to focus on open-ended questions (e.g., "Why don't you describe your customer service process?" or "What are some of the delivery problems you have been having?"). I sometimes believe that is overemphasized. I agree that these are the best questions to stimulate the thought processes of others. But don't forget to ask good closed-ended questions when you wish to affirm or confirm a particular point that the other party has made. For example, assume you are speaking to a customer who says, "Your materials must arrive at our factory by Friday, June 14, in order for us to meet our production deadlines." You might simply state, "Let me make sure I understand. Friday, June 14, is a "must-deliver-by" date for us, otherwise you will not make your deadlines—correct?" If you ask a good closed-ended question at the proper time, you validate their point and clarify that you heard it correctly. This, in turn, can cut down on misunderstandings.

Take great notes. One of my biggest listening faults is that I trust too much to memory (This from a person who has difficulty remembering the title of the last movie he saw or what he had for lunch yesterday!). I encourage you to take good notes in your significant conversations. When you open the conversation, let the other person know you plan to take notes and ask their approval to do so. Of course, if you meet with someone regularly, as I do in my executive coaching practice, it may only be necessary to mention note-taking in the first meeting.

Remember, though, to use caution when note-taking. Be careful that you do not use inappropriate body language, sighs, mumblings, or other noises or nervous reactions that create negative vibrations when you are taking notes. And remember to still maintain eye contact and ask questions while taking your notes.

One final thought about note-taking. If you have a behavior style like I do, and do not do well at note-taking, bring along a colleague who takes excellent notes! You can also ask permission to record the conversation.

This is not an exhaustive list of all the skills you can employ if you wish to be a good listener or a better listener, but if you work on strengthening listening skills, you will be a better worker, boss, partner, parent, son or daughter, or spouse. You will be a better person.

And just as my grandson was unaware of my observing him, we are also being continually observed. Put yourself in the place of those with whom you come into contact. How would your listening skills measure up? Are you giving the impression of inattentive, unconcerned listening? Or are you displaying active and genuine hearing? Perceptions play a significant role in our dealings with others. Bettering your skills as a listener is sure to be an advantage throughout life.

CHAPTER 7

———

LEADERSHIP

The term leadership is everywhere. We hear it, we read it, we practice it, and we judge others on their ability to lead. For a word that is used so often, do we know what it means? Have we defined it for ourselves?

There are many accepted definitions of leadership from a multitude of sources. As such, I believe most of us have our own opinions regarding leadership. We think we know what makes a good leader—someone we might emulate; someone we would follow. We know what we like and dislike about the leaders in our life. We have an idea of how we would lead if we were given the opportunity. If you are currently in a leadership position, regardless of the size of your team, what would your team say about your leadership abilities? Would their opinions match yours? Would their definition of leadership be consistent with your own?

There are leaders for every area of our life: personal, professional, recreational, spiritual, etc. Leadership characteristics will differ in their application in these different backgrounds, but most of them are consistent, no matter the role the leader may take.

Years ago, as I prepared for a presentation I was to give on leadership, I challenged myself to create at least one leadership attribute for each letter of the alphabet. Sounds easy, right? Wrong! This activity proved much more complicated than I originally expected. It forced me to think beyond the traditional six or eight attributes that quickly came to mind when I defined leadership.

As I set myself to the task, I admit I included some thoughts I borrowed from others. Those borrowed, I have recognized with an appropriate reference. In some cases, several attributes for a specific letter came to mind, so I have listed multiples. At the end of this chapter, I share my personal definition of a leader and I challenge you to create your own. You cannot lead if you don't have an idea in your mind of what leadership is. And you certainly will not follow a leader who does not live up to your own definition. I hope my thoughts help provoke your own thinking about good leadership and how you will choose to lead going forward.

You may find it advantageous to read this list at least three times. The first time through just read what is printed. The second time, I challenge you to develop your own definition of leadership and assess your own leadership qualities against that definition. How many of these traits do you possess? How many would you like to possess? Do you demonstrate these on a daily basis? If someone else was to assess your leadership ability using this list what type of conclusions would they draw regarding your leadership ability?

The third time reading through this list, think of those around you that lead. Do they live up to your definition of a leader? You can't change the leaders around you, but you can change who you choose to follow. If you don't have strong leaders in your life you may find it beneficial to seek others.

Remember, leadership is not easy. Many can lead, but few can do it very well.

Accountable. A leader holds herself accountable first, then holds others accountable fairly and equally to achieve their tasks.

Brainstorm. A leader is open to the ideas of others and will listen to them when offered.

Caring. A leader cares about herself and her people.

Change. A leader is able to lead through change. One constant in life is change. It will always be there; it will always be happening. A leader will know how to navigate change.

Clarity. A leader delivers the message clearly, regardless of the medium. A leader seeks clarity, communicates with clarity, thinks with clarity, and provides clarity of direction.

Coaching. A leader knows when to seek help or assistance for himself or one of his team through coaching. He also knows when to be a coach to others.

Communicate. A leader is committed to open and continuous communication, in various mediums. She is consistent in communicating the results of both her personal and her team's attempts, achievements, and failures. A leader also recognizes that communication is a two-way street and listens very well.

Compromise. A leader listens to other points of view and is willing to balance his opinion with others to arrive at mutually acceptable solutions. But this leader also recognizes that at times he cannot compromise for the good of himself, his team, or the organization.

Creativity (or Innovation). A leader recognizes the need for an organization or a team to stimulate new ideas to continue to grow and be successful. She promotes an environment that is willing to try new things, new ideas, new processes, etc. While she might not possess a strong creative gene, she understands the importance of looking at new ideas that can stimulate growth.

Culture. A leader understands the importance of a culture that is consistent throughout the organization. He fulfills the culture by living it and setting the example for others. He walks the talk.

Developer. A leader develops others and builds a succession plan with qualified people. He encourages them to challenge the norm. He doesn't fear surrounding himself with people who are smarter than he is.

Diplomacy. A leader tactfully balances relationships with her board, other leaders, peers, employees, customers, vendors, and other stakeholders.

Emotional Intelligence. A leader knows who she is; she is aware of her own feelings, and is aware and respectful of the feelings of others. She knows how to manage her emotions and her relationships with others.

Energy. A leader brings a high energy level to his work and his team. He is able to motivate people to action and knows how and when to have fun. He understands that he must take care of his physical self to have the energy needed.

Encourager. A leader constantly encourages similar behaviors in the people she leads. She is able to step out of the way to allow others to perform.

Ethical. A leader believes in doing the right thing—always and no matter what. He does the right thing regardless of who is watching.

Example. A leader understands the importance of walking the talk and will do so consistently.

Feedback. A leader does not fear being vulnerable. He seeks feedback, accepts it openly, and responds appropriately. He also provides feedback frequently and fairly.

Feedforward. The feedforward principle focuses on the future—what can we do to be better. A leader practices this skill along with traditional feedback. I learned this principle from a presentation by, and the writings of, Marshall Goldsmith. We will discuss this more in depth in chapter 9.

Flexible. A leader is flexible, by recognizing the need for change and flexing as needed.

Follower. A leader should be a good follower when necessary. She can sit on the bus behind the driver—someone else more experienced or more knowledgeable—to drive through unusual or unfamiliar terrain. She recognizes that sometimes she must step aside and let another lead for a specific purpose.

Gratitude. A leader recognizes that everyone in the organization has a role and shows thankfulness for the contributions of those that work for him. When someone fulfills their role, he thanks them.

Greatness. A leader always recognizes this attribute in others first; then, she recognizes it in herself. She sees the greatness in everyone who works with her and encourages others to achieve greatness in their role. A leader rewards both individuals and teams when they have accomplished their tasks.

Humility. A leader knows his rank in the organization, but doesn't need to flaunt it to everyone. While he is confident and self-assured, he does not need to take credit for everything. He is aware of the contribution of everyone around him. In addition, when a humble leader recognizes that an organization needs a specific leadership trait or skill that he does not possess or practice well, he is not afraid to go out and find the appropriate resource to build that strength into the team. He willingly surrounds himself with people who possess skills or talents stronger than his.

Humor. A leader knows when to laugh and encourages laughter in others. She sees the humor in situations. She also knows when humor is inappropriate.

Integrity. A leader does what she says she will do, and she holds others accountable to do what they say they will do.

Intuition. In "Numbers" below, I posit that a good leader knows when and how to use data and analytics in making decisions. That same leader also is willing to act on intuition. She's confident to act on her natural ability to know something without it necessarily being supported by evidence, or having been proven in the past.

Just. A leader treats everyone fairly and clearly communicates his beliefs of fairness, honesty, and integrity.

Knowledge. A leader possesses it, seeks it, and does not fear or envy others that may have more. As previously stated, he does not need to be the smartest person in the room.

Learner. A leader is a lifelong learner. He learns from and respects history, but does not live it. A leader enjoys learning new things and adapting new knowledge to his own style.

Limitations. A leader knows her limitations. She knows when she needs to get help and she seeks it out. She knows when her team or her people are stretched beyond their own abilities and she takes appropriate action to find the necessary resources to help. She also recognizes that understanding limitations, whether in herself or her people, might require severe action. She takes that action appropriately.

Listen. A leader knows how to listen. She practices the best listening skills and encourages the same in her team and those around her.

Manners. A leader says, "Please" and "Thank you" and treats others with respect.

Mentoring. A leader serves as a mentor to help others find their own way in their education, their careers, or lives.

Moderate. A leader practices moderation in all facets of his life and the business. He works hard, fervently, passionately. But, he also knows when to relax, take a breather, and re-energize. He expects the same of others and encourages them to do so.

Moral. A leader has her own set of moral standards which she has developed over her lifetime. She lives according to these standards and applies them fairly and consistently in her dealings with others.

Numbers. A leader understands that data and analytics are important contributors to success, but she is not married to them. She expects to have systems and processes which capture relevant information and measure outcomes. She uses data to assist in making decisions, but is also willing to accept new ideas, even if the facts may not indicate it.

Opinionated. A leader knows when to hold to his opinion and when to stick to his beliefs. But, he also knows when to compromise.

Organized. A leader appreciates the need for structure and process to exist in her own life and in the life of the organization. She also understands that too much structure can stifle an organization or a team.

Passion. A leader has a strong desire for the success of the organization. He believes in its vision and mission and encourages everyone else to be similarly engaged. A leader fosters an environment that promotes passion.

Persistent. A leader sets goals and maintains a steadfast course of action to achieve them. She is willing to modify the goals or change course along the way. A leader recognizes that the most effectively designed plan will change immediately upon implementation.

Plan. A leader has a plan and communicates it—again and again. A leader monitors his plan and changes it when the circumstances require.

Quizzical/Questioning. A leader seeks new information and new ideas. She has a curiosity for learning and asks good, relevant questions. She encourages the same in all of the people with whom she works. She is not afraid to challenge the status quo and is not offended when challenged.

Respect. A leader recognizes the worth in each and every individual and honors their worth by treating them fairly and with dignity. He demonstrates trust so that others will trust him. A leader does not expect others to do things the way that he does. He does, however, expect them to treat others the way that they would have others treat them. He holds himself and everyone else to that standard.

Responsibility. A leader takes responsibility for her actions and expects others to do the same. She understands what her role and responsibilities are in the organization and she knows when to take action. She communicates the roles and responsibilities of others with clarity.

Risk. A leader is fearless about taking appropriate risks. He evaluates the positives and negatives of a situation, weighs the risk factors, and analyzes relevant data measuring the risk. He is not afraid to take risks or make risky decisions.

Self-awareness/Self-esteem/Self-respect. A leader knows who she is. She knows her values and lives by them. A leader understands her strengths and weaknesses. She understands her capabilities, limitations, and potential.

Self-confidence. A leader has a strong sense of self-worth and his own capacity to achieve. He is not afraid to make and defend his own decisions.

Self-development. A leader takes the necessary steps to build her own strengths through additional education or training. She encourages the same attribute in her team and helps them find the right avenues to obtain further development.

Stimulator. Not all great leaders are Creative or Innovators, but they are people who can stimulate others to create and innovate.

Strategic. A leader understands the business beyond just her own area of responsibility. She understands the potential impact that her decisions will make on other people and parts of the organization. She also understands the impact of her decisions on the community and world around her organization.

Steward. A leader is a good steward. He strives to build a place that is better than when he entered it.

Supportive. A leader provides support to the members of his team; he understands the resources, tools, training, and development they need and helps ensure that they are received by all employees. A leader serves as both a mentor and a coach.

Think Straight and Talk Straight. (Come on, you didn't think I could let a list go by without this one!) A leader thinks straight. She gets the relevant facts, understands the context, avoids the noise and fluff, keeps it simple, applies logic, and decides and acts on her decisions. She talks straight; she tells it like it is, keeps it simple, considers the perspective of others, and affirms that she is understood. She is courteous and respectful and manages her emotions throughout.

Teamwork/Team builder. A leader understands the importance of teamwork and how to build high-performance teams. He creates an environment in which everyone works together toward a common goal.

Trust. A leader creates trust by being trustworthy. She exemplifies it for others and holds others accountable to demonstrate their own trustworthiness.

Understanding. A leader should "Seek first to understand, then to be understood." He wants to know how things work, how they fit together, how the processes are effective. But, most of all, he seeks to understand the people. He wants to know what they think and how they feel.

He wants to know their issues. He wants to understand all aspects of the organization's environment in addition to the environment outside the organization so he can be prepared for change.

Visionary. A leader has a strong belief in what the organization can be and has a personal belief in what she can be within that organization.

Wisdom. A leader usually doesn't credit himself with having wisdom. He prefers to recognize it in others. He can't really define it, but he knows it when he sees it.

X (The Unknown). A leader learns to deal with and solve for the unknown. She controls that which she can and worries not about that which she cannot control.[10]

Y (Why?). A leader asks "Y"? Mr. Sakichi Toyoda, the founder of Toyota Industries developed a "5 Whys" question-and-answer technique during the evolution of its manufacturing methodologies.[11] The primary goal of the technique is to determine the root cause of a problem by repeating the question "why". The questioner keeps asking why until the real cause of the problem or issue is uncovered.[12]

Zeal. A leader approaches all she does with bridled enthusiasm. She doesn't carry her zeal to extremes, but she knows when to demonstrate it openly.

While it is easy to formulate a list of leadership traits, it is more difficult to create an extensive list with a definition of each trait. As you can see, the list here is extensive. While you may excel at some of these attributes, there are many more here that when strengthened can make you a better leader.

Although my list of leadership traits is long, my definition of a leader is simple: **A leader creates an environment in which people willingly work together to achieve a common goal.**

My definition of a leader is straightforward because leadership itself is straightforward. Although an effective leader possesses many of the traits listed here, the act of leading is simple: create an environment in which people willingly work together to achieve a common goal.

As you think about leadership, I challenge you to develop your own personal definition. Once defined, you will be able to measure yourself and your success as a leader. Devote some time to focus on what is important to developing your own leadership style. What are the attributes of a good leader? If you wish to lead well, what character-istics should you possess? What habits do you need in order to feel comfortable in your own "leadership shoes"? What is your definition of a leader? Are you living up to it? What more can you do to increase your confidence in your own leadership ability?

One of the characteristics mentioned is moderation. It is important that we do not take some of these leadership characteristics to an ex-treme. For example, have you ever had the opportunity to work with someone who wanted to change everything all of the time? Someone who created an environment that was committed more to the idea of change for the sake of change rather than to achieve a new, more mean-ingful goal? Alternatively, while it is important for a leader to maintain a steady hand on the throttle of leadership, there are some who commit to such steadiness or past success that they don't recognize the need to respond to the changes in the environment around them. Adopting the belief and behavior of moderation in all things will help leaders recog-nize the need to moderate appropriately and help maintain balance.

My leadership list is not all-inclusive. As I mentioned earlier, one sim-ply needs to go to a bookstore and see the shelves filled with leadership books to realize how many different perspectives exist on leadership and the attributes of a good leader. To anyone who leads, my recom-mendation is to gather your own thoughts on the key characteristics you believe are relevant to fulfilling your leadership role—whether you are leading a small team or a global organization. Then, go out and fulfill them.

Throughout my career, I have had the opportunity to work with both effective and ineffective leaders. I am sure you can attest to the same. At different times in my life, I have also been a better leader than at others. This list of leadership attributes helps me think about the type of leader I want to be. As a leader, it is important to remember that there is always room for improvement. I encourage you to use this list and this chapter as a reference throughout your career. Refer to it ev-ery now and again. Use it as a form of checks and balances to see how you are doing. Pick a few attributes and challenge yourself to journal regularly how you are performing against those attributes. When you have made them habits and are satisfied that they are embedded in your daily leadership life, pick a few more and repeat the process. I am confident that this will help you and it will not take long for you to see your growth as a leader.

CHAPTER 8

A COMMUNICATION PROCESS

After the financial upheaval during the first decade of this century, there was much expositing in various arenas (webinars, emails, digital and print media, etc.) on the idea of "The Tone at the Top." The focus of these messages dealt primarily with ethical issues and how to communicate them from executives to others throughout an organization.

I believe that leadership in every organization is responsible for setting the appropriate tone, vision, strategy or culture. Once the tone is set, what happens next? How effectively is the tone communicated and reinforced throughout the organization?

Within any type of organization—corporate, not-for-profit, team, division, department—the leader has the responsibility to communicate to his organizational team. If his organization is within a larger organization, he also has the responsibility to make certain that the communication is consistent with that which is communicated from above. Leadership should establish this regular line of communication related to all information that should be transmitted throughout the business—culture, strategies, vision, mission, policies, processes, etc.

Let me use an example of a significant change that was made in the accounting and finance arena several years ago—the implementation of every accountant and internal auditor's favorite piece of legislation— Sarbanes-Oxley (SOX).

Before I go any further, if you are reading this chapter and you have an accounting or finance background, you probably know more about SOX than I do. On the other hand, if you do not have that background, do not worry. This chapter is not trying to help you understand the legislation and the rules it created. This chapter is about communicating significant topics throughout your organization in a fashion that is both consistent and understandable.

In brief, SOX was designed to help companies improve their internal controls. Part of the guidance for implementation stated: "The chief executive officer is ultimately responsible and should assume 'ownership' of the system (of internal controls). More than any other individual, the chief executive sets the 'tone at the top' that affects integrity and ethics and other factors of a positive control environment.[13]

As a result of this legislation, every public company has completed huge documentation projects related to internal controls. Thousands of accountants, internal auditors, and consultants wrote up procedures, created checklists, and testing and reporting procedures. While all of this activity was taking place, I found myself wondering "How many leaders thought about communicating the reasons for this effort to the employees of the company?" So, I tried to find out the answer to that simple question.

On a number of different occasions, I asked individuals and teams who worked for public companies:

- Have you heard of Sarbanes-Oxley?

- Do you know how or why it is being implemented in your company?

- Have you received any communication about the need for a strong internal control process?

- Has your company ever told you how a strong internal control process can help you in your job?

Of this small (admittedly, non-statistical) population, only two in seven people responded that they had ever heard of Sarbanes-Oxley and the need for internal control processes and documentation. I couldn't believe it. How did so few people know about a change that affected every public company everywhere?

You can also do a simple test. Has your company instituted a significant process change in the recent past? Pick a step related to that process. Talk to an employee or team member that is supposed to complete this

part of the process and ask them if they understand why they are doing the step. I hope the response you receive shows that the employee
understood the purpose of the change and the benefit of it and isn't just
going through the motions without understanding why.

Better yet, try this. Does your organization promote or espouse a list
of key points of organizational culture, or a list of "corporate values"?
Perhaps they appear on company posters, whiteboards, and the website? Randomly stop different employees and ask them which of the
company values is the most important to them. Ask them how they
model this value in their work or how they see it modeled by others. I
bet you will be surprised by the answers you receive.

So why is communication within an organization so important? Why
do I feel so strongly that each employee understands what is happening? The success of any business is enhanced when each employee understands how he or she fits in. This applies to every communication
issue—strategy, vision, process change, culture, etc. Employees must
take responsibility for their portion of each of these areas. They must
own them. But they cannot take responsibility if they don't understand
it. They can't live it if they are kept in the dark about it. It is up to
each leader, throughout the organization, to shine a light through good
communication and feedback.

Failure to regularly and consistently communicate within an organization or your team creates a "communication fog" or lack of clarity.
If there is a lack of clarity, both leaders and employees begin making
interpretations of their own. Once people begin to make their own
interpretations of policies, strategies, or even vision, they will behave
accordingly. In addition, they drive behavior of others according to
those interpretations. This can result in behavior that is inconsistent
with the initial intent of the communication. As inconsistent behavior
permeates the organization, nothing short of chaos will arise. This results in lost productivity, frustration, deterioration in morale, or even
inappropriate actions. And it all occurs because communication was
not initiated or made clear. It is not only important in communication
to set the tone from the top, it is imperative to communicate and reinforce it regularly, and to include appropriate processes for feedback up
and down the lines of communication.

It is my assumption that many of you reading this book have implemented quality control programs, strategic plans, and information

systems over the years. Chances are, if your communication was poor, your implementation was as well. However, I would bet that if your communication was good, your implementation was successful. Wouldn't you agree that one element of your success was to make sure that those affected by these changes understood what was happening and why? You answered the many "why" questions. "Why do I have to do this?" "Why are we changing this process?" "Why me?" "Why now?" And you didn't stop there. Once the procedures were implemented, you continued to communicate consistently in accordance with the answers you gave during the change process.

Any corporation that desires to maximize the benefits of a process or system change must communicate the reason and benefits for the change repeatedly. Employees want to know "What's in it for me?" (Often referred to as the WIIFM factor.) Once they understand WIIFM, they are more committed and more likely to modify their behavior.

Any major communication within your organization—vision, mission, strategy, process change, organizational change, etc.—should be based on a communication plan related to the change. The plan should describe the nature of the communication, the responsibility of each level of leadership to communicate it, the tools to be used and the timing to be followed. So next time you need to communicate a message, whether it is vision, mission, strategy, or process (such as internal controls), I recommend you follow these easy steps listed below.

Step 1. Let's assume an overall strategy has been developed and the appropriate leadership group has signed off on it. The CEO should prepare an initial message to all employees. The opening message will clearly and simply state the strategy—what it is, why it is important, and how it will be implemented. She should express her commitment to it and the support it has from the board of directors and the senior leadership team. She should also be clear about her (and their) commitment to this process. Periodically, there should be successive messages from her that identify the progress being made to achieve the strategy. It is also a good idea to highlight specific, positive results that occur from implementation and reward individual employees or groups who make a positive contribution to its success. Additionally, it is important to acknowledge those situations in which the strategy did not work successfully and had to be changed, or was scrapped.

Step 2. As a part of her regular meetings and communications with her senior executive team, she must inform them of their responsibilities—not only about the strategy itself, but also about the communication process they should develop in their own parts of the organization. The message content that they deliver will focus on their area of responsibility to achieve the strategy, but it will also be consistent with the overall communications about the strategy from the top. The process should include regular feedback to her on the progress of strategy implementation. Systematic reports should be simply designed to flow through the organizational structure and reinforce the message.

Step 3. The senior executive team should then guide successive teams below them to initiate a similar process within their own areas of responsibility. They must communicate their own strategy for their functional area. It must support the overall strategy, and they should make sure the employees understand how it does. They should communicate the importance and value of it to the success of their operation. They should explain why it is important for each employee to take their responsibility for understanding and implementing the strategy seriously. They should also discuss the consequences that may occur if the strategy is not successfully implemented.

Step 4. Employees at all levels should be given time to understand what is communicated to them about the strategy. They should be encouraged to ask questions. They should be challenged to offer ideas and suggestions to successfully implement it. They should be rewarded and acknowledged when they do. They should be held appropriately accountable when they do not. They should be encouraged to provide feedback to their leaders about issues they see around the strategy implementation. In addition to encouraging feedback, a process should be in place to regularly capture feedback. The process can include ideas such as suggestion programs, regularly scheduled team feedback meetings, town hall meetings, use of internal social media sites or simply encouraging leaders to periodically discuss important communications within their teams to obtain feedback.

I met a department manager in the manufacturing industry that took this one step further. He told me that it wasn't just important that employees see the record of success. When they had a lost time accident, he brought the team of production employees from the area together to discuss what could be done to eliminate the risk of a similar accident in the future. This young leader realized that in a manufacturing environment, things were going to happen that were safety risks.

It wasn't just important to communicate the results of the successes. It was also important to discuss the failures and get employee input on how to minimize them in the future. His communication with his employees was consistent and this was obvious in the results of the department. Their safety record improved and employees began to call out each other when safety standards were not met or were about to be "short-cutted."

Any communication plan should at least include steps similar to those above to ensure the flow up and down and across the organization. Some other things I have learned over the years about communication are:

Form. The form of your messages can vary. Messages can be delivered by email, bulletin boards, newsletters, texting, social media sites, websites, or face-to-face meetings. I recommend adapting some parts of all of these communication vehicles in your organization. As a part of implementing a significant new strategy, I observed one company that conducted separate information sessions in a town-hall format to make sure that everyone was apprised of the new or revised direction. This is an excellent step to bring all employees to the same understanding of the strategy and its benefit to each and every employee. Use whatever method of employee communication is effective within your company. Of course, you have to consider the cost of delivering these messages. But, you also must consider the cost of not doing so. And as leaders, you must remember that just because you say it once does not necessarily mean it was heard or that it will be done.

Some organizations post strategy messages in public—often as a part of their marketing and advertising. As a part of the overall communication plan, I like this style, but I also realize it doesn't fit everyone. Take a look at the messages, expectations, strategies, and vision that are posted in the facilities of successful athletic teams. They make their point with very few words. One of my favorite public business messages was when Ford Motor Company said: "Quality is Job 1." What about that can you not understand? It is important to remind your employees of where your organization is going and how they fit in.

Manufacturing plants are a great example of public messages. In the manufacturing industry, safety is always a key concern. If a company has an objective to minimize lost time accidents, signs are posted around the facility. "It has been 73 days since our last lost time accident. Thanks to all of you for keeping this in mind as you work."

Repetition. I do not believe you can over-communicate key topics related to culture, vision, mission, strategy, etc. Be creative. Deliver such messages in a variety of ways so as not to diminish the importance of the message because of repetition—but repetition is necessary. Repetition always contributes to better communication.

Reinforcement. Initial communications to employees should help them understand the overall strategy and how it fits into their daily efforts to be successful in the company. Regular messages from a leader to outside stakeholders or employees, whether delivered in a group session, internal newsletters, quotations on emails, etc. should be consistent with the overall plan. I once worked with a company in which the CEO had the stated values of the company—five of them—listed in the top margin or header of every meeting agenda he held. Electronic communication systems, websites, and internal social media are great tools to accomplish this also.

As time goes on, communications should include stories about strategic successes or failures. These are invaluable to help employees understand what is learned from both. Employees are better equipped to do their jobs if they see how the results impact the strategy going forward. The content of the messages should be tailored to the specific audience (e.g., department, division, sector, etc.); however, the effect on cross-functions should not be overlooked. For example, you wouldn't tell the IT employees about how the strategy has been successfully implemented in the shipping department, but you would tell both the IT employees and the shipping department employees how an element of the strategy that affects both of them has been successfully implemented. Or, if the shipping department employees developed a unique manner in which to communicate or implement strategy to its employees, you might want to share that idea with your IT employees, or for that matter, you should share the idea with all of your employees.

Another great example comes from my experience with a company in the direct sales business. This company had a significant telephone sales service center. Each group within the center had specific goals related to things like sales calls made, dollar sales generated, etc. Whenever someone or some department hit a special target, the person responsible got up from their desk and rang a ship's bell that was hanging on the wall in the department. And, on those days, or sequential days in which targets were not met, the leader brought the teams together to talk about what was happening and why they were slipping below expectations.

Clarity. Clarity is also a critical feature of the communication process. Too often, company leadership delivers messages with vague assumptions or directives. One of my favorites is: "This new (strategy, process, product, or service—pick your choice) will help us take our organization to the next level." What is "the next level"? Why is this advancement important? Vague directives fail to provide clarity and lack specific action steps. They assume the recipients will understand and comply. Later, they are surprised when employees did not understand or comply. Messages about strategy implementation need to be straightforward and complete. They get to the point; they make the point. They reflect my "Think Straight. Talk Straight." mantra.

Non-verbals. Another aspect of communication relates to the way you communicate indirectly. We discussed this in the Listening chapter and the key points hold true here as well. Do you create the impression that communications coming to you regarding policy, strategy, etc. are meaningless or worthless to you in your role in the company? If your boss or leader is relating some aspect of strategy or direction and you are fiddling with your iPhone or rolling your eyes or making faces at one of your peers, what are you communicating? If you don't agree with communication coming to you, you have a responsibility to yourself and your team to address the issue. Or, what if one of your colleagues is communicating a negative message indirectly? What do you do about it? You should take a moment—tactfully and diplomatically—to hold that person accountable. Regardless of your title or position it is imperative that you lead by example. Your words and actions should always be consistent with the message you are trying to convey. If you want to earn the respect of those you lead, you have to walk the talk.

No matter what you communicate (vision, mission, value statements, expectations, directional changes, etc.), you cannot communicate too much. Whether you are a leader, a manager, or an employee, recognize your responsibility to own your share of the organization's communications. Deliver the message consistently; ask for and provide feedback regularly. Even when you feel like you are over-communicating, communicate again.

Regardless of the message, the leader sets it at the top and is responsible to communicate it down through the organization. The leader must also ensure that communications below the top are appropriately fed back up to the top. This builds and reinforces the message and strengthens its consistency throughout the organization. It is important that you own your share of any communication and how you communicate that share also has an impact on the culture. We will discuss this further in the chapter on culture. If you believe in the communication that comes to you, then it is your responsibility to own it, support it and communicate it to others. If you don't believe the communication is accurate or appropriate, it is your responsibility to feed that back also.

Finally, because I have said it over and over, I will say it again. You cannot communicate too much. Clear and consistent communication with everyone involved improves understanding, increases commitment and yields better results.

CHAPTER 9

———

FEEDBACK

In previous chapters we have discussed the importance of communication and, to that regard, the necessity of listening. Yet we cannot fully understand communication until we cover another key aspect: feedback. As you read this chapter, I encourage you to Think Straight. Talk Straight. as feedback is much more effective when clear and concise.

I have heard Ken Blanchard, the American author and management expert, say "Feedback is the breakfast of champions." So why then would most of us rather skip breakfast than give or receive feedback?

Many of you reading this book are in some level of leadership role within your organization. You lead a company, a business unit, a division, a functional area, or a team. In that role, you have a responsibility to help develop the people working for you. In order to do this, you have to give them feedback. How you give feedback, and ultimately how individuals receive it, will directly impact their performance. People that feel good about themselves will produce good results. People that feel negatively about themselves will produce less than ideal results. As a leader, which would you rather have?

Most organizations have a structured review process. It is not my purpose here to challenge or change them. But I will offer you a communication suggestion or two that have helped me over the years. One of my basic assumptions in writing this chapter is that when we discuss performance issues with others, we tend to focus on the weaknesses or deficiencies in our subordinate's performance. Generally, there is nothing wrong with this approach, as we want people to build their skills in certain areas. As you have these discussions, I suggest you consider the two techniques I describe later.

Let me share a personal example. Many, many years ago, when I was working in the accounting profession, most of my clients were in the retail and wholesale distribution businesses. As I set the stage for this story, please recognize that these were days when most business people wore full business dress—for men this meant suits, dress shirts, and ties. The nature and style of the dress tended to vary with the industry.

It was time for my annual review. I was performing very well. My evaluation reflected that I had met or exceeded expectations. The reviewer's comments were very positive. Then, near the end of my review, he commented, "One thing you should really work on is your dress code. You wear suits that look a bit "loud," and they also do not favor your physical characteristics (admittedly, I was on the heavier side of my lifetime weight curve in those days). You really should invest in a nice, dark pin stripe suit. You will look much more professional." After the review was over, which was primarily very positive, what do you think I thought about the most? Which comment was I hung up on? Well, I will tell you this. I did not think about the various behaviors that I was doing well. I did not celebrate my great review. No. Instead, I went home and reviewed my closet. It was full of reasonably expensive suits and they did have a panoply of patterns and colors. In fact, I was pretty proud of my combinations of light suits, dark shirts and wide ties with varied patterns and colors. Many of my clients were dressed in similar fashion. Though upon reflection, I had to admit that client personnel who were working in the respective accounting and finance departments of these companies were a bit more toned down. I began to wonder if the comment was directed at my suit pattern and color selection, or whether my reviewer felt I was carrying too much weight!

After giving it more thought, I discussed this review at home with my wife. I acknowledged that the suggestion was a reasonably well-intended one, although the delivery might have been a bit clumsy, and I did modify my future clothing selections. I also modified my diet and exercise patterns and dropped several pounds. What I still remember most about that particular review, and what rankled me the most, was the way the idea was presented. It was delivered as more of a command than a suggestion; more of a personal critique (that I felt in the moment was unsupported) than a recommendation to improve. Instead of building me up, this feedback left me feeling deflated and unmotivated.

When done properly, feedback is very effective and is a necessary component for growth. However, just because it is necessary does not mean it is always easy to give or receive. As I hope you see from my example, even well-intended feedback, given poorly, can have a negative impact. Without feedback, we are much more likely to remain stagnant and stuck in our ways. Feedback gives us the opportunity to learn, change, grow, and, ultimately, to increase productivity.

Unfortunately, most individuals dread feedback on both sides. It is rare that you see an individual brimming with excitement knowing they will be giving or receiving feedback. However, I think feedback has a bad reputation. It is not because it is not useful, but because it is often done incorrectly or poorly. People take it personally, feelings get hurt, and productivity, in many instances, actually drops.

So I challenge you to make a commitment to change how you deliver feedback, and consequently, how it is received. By making a few changes, you can help make feedback positive and effective. Here are a couple of coaching techniques that you can use as you conduct reviews with others. I believe they are effective and can be used in a variety of situations.

The first technique is called "feedforward." Mentioned in an earlier chapter, the idea of feedforward comes from an experienced leadership development educator and executive coach by the name of Marshall Goldsmith. On his website, www.marshallgoldsmithlibrary.com, he offers a free paper titled "*Try FeedForward Instead of Feedback.*"[14] I won't repeat the entire article here, although I strongly encourage you to read it. A few key points in executing feedforward in a review situation include the following:

- As a part of your review discussion, ask the person to consider their overall evaluation and think about one or two behaviors that they would like to change that they believe would improve their performance. Have them state those desired changes to you.

  Rather than providing instruction on how to change that behavior or how to do better, rather than agreeing what that "negative" behavior has looked like in the past, give them two suggestions on how they might change that behavior going forward. Better yet, encourage them to think of two ways they might modify their approach in the future. Help them construct a sample sce-

nario and plan how their behavior might look different. For example, they might say: "I have been told that I have a tendency
to interrupt people before they complete their thought. I might
even finish their sentences for them." Ask them if they recall a
specific example. Whether they do or not, you might say something like:

- The next time you feel yourself jumping into the conversation
  to offer your own perspective, take a deep breath and make sure
  that they have completed their thought. You might even consider repeating or reframing the thought back to them to ensure
  that you have heard it correctly.

- Let a couple of seconds of silence pass and then ask if they have
  anything more to say on the topic.

- If you think this is a habit you use often in meetings, have a close
  personal colleague observe you during meetings and note when
  you do this.

Additionally, Goldsmith recites eleven reasons why feedforward is a
more effective technique than feedback. Some of his reasons that resonate with me are:

- People can change the future. They cannot change the past. So
  why dwell on it?

- It can be more productive to help people "get it right" than to
  point out how "they are wrong."

- People take feedforward more positively than traditional feedback.

Another feedback technique worth trying comes from the coaching
and consulting world. Known as "appreciative inquiry," Coaching
Leaders Ltd. described this technique in a briefing paper as one that focuses on changing an organization or an individual in a non-tradition-
al fashion.[15] Traditionally, we seek to help others change by attempting to solve a problem or an issue with their behavior in the past. For
example, through appreciative inquiry, the coach or consultant works
with the individual to help them understand what is working about
their current behavior or performance and build on that for the future.

The coach doesn't ask traditional feedback questions such as:

- What went wrong and how can we fix it going forward?

- Why do you suppose that approach did not work?

Instead, the leader asks:

- What works for you in most of these situations and how could that be applied to this situation?

- What can you do to make this situation better or to improve on what you are trying to accomplish?

- Think about situations you have resolved in the past—what worked and how can you apply that technique to solve this?

- If you agree this is an area to improve, what will success look like to you when you achieve it?

In my experience, the primary benefit of both the feedforward approach and the appreciative inquiry technique is this—they help build relationships with others. It is far better to help someone change behavior by looking to the future versus dwelling on an unsuccessful behavior from the past. Earlier in this chapter I told a story about some feedback I was given that I did not receive very well. I also believe these techniques are effective when the person receiving the feedback objects to it or does not think it is appropriate or fair. Like anyone else, I do not like to be told that I did not perform up to expectations, or that the result of my work was not satisfactory. For example, I have mentioned elsewhere in this book that I have a health condition to manage. I am a Type 2 diabetic. Several years ago, my primary physician would examine me, bluntly tell me I was not managing my condition well, insist that I work harder on it and often prescribe another medication. If I have not met my goals with my current doctor, his usual reaction is simply something like this: "OK. What are you going to do about it over the next six months? How are you going to correct or change your habits to manage it better? Is there anything else I can do to help you focus on this more properly?" He does not criticize or scold me for bad behavior. He has me focus on the future and create future expectations to work towards. Consequently, I am more open to change because he is not critiquing my behavior.

I strongly encourage you to practice either or both of these techniques when working with your teams in your leadership role. I am confident that the results will be better when you focus on future performance and stop dwelling on past behaviors. I also believe that if you employ either technique in the more formal setting of an annual performance review, that it elevates the quality of the conversation. It builds stronger relationships with your team members. Both techniques can also be used when coaching or mentoring or even when working with customers or clients to help solve problems. By applying the techniques discussed in this chapter, you will see a positive change. If you still have an interest in learning more about either of these techniques, I recommend:

- For feedforward, Google *Marshall Goldsmith Library* and click on "Free Resources."

- For appreciative inquiry, Google that term and research to your heart's content.

I am confident that these techniques will help you build skills as a leader and in your interactions with others. As you employ these new techniques, be conscious of the reactions and results that you are seeing. I believe they will both be favorable, and hopefully both you and those with whom you share feedback will have a more positive outlook toward receiving feedback.

CHAPTER 10

———

EMOTIONS AND ATTITUDE

Has anyone ever told you that you have a bad attitude? How about a good attitude? Have you ever felt emotionally out of control? Did anyone ever tell you that you were on an emotional roller coaster?

After many decades of dealing with my own emotions and attitudes and also observing the emotions and attitudes of others, I believe the topics of emotions and attitude are linked. One's attitude towards something or someone is formed by the emotions one has experienced when dealing with that something or someone. Since they are more together than separate, I have addressed them together in one chapter.

Our emotions and attitude affect us every day. They are expressed both internally and externally, and they affect our thoughts as well as our actions. Learning how to manage our emotions and attitude can improve our overall outlook and help us to become better leaders. With this in mind, let's look first at emotions and their roles in our lives.

Emotions

Dictionary.com defines emotion as:

1. an affective state of consciousness in which joy, sorrow, fear, hate, or the like, is experienced, as distinguished from cognitive and volitional states of consciousness.

2. any of the feelings of joy, sorrow, fear, hate, love, etc.

3. any strong agitation of the feelings actuated by experiencing love, hate, fear, etc., and usually accompanied by certain physiological changes, as increased heartbeat or respiration, and often

overt manifestation, as crying or shaking.

4. an instance of this.

5. something that causes such a reaction (e.g., the powerful emotion of a great symphony).[16]

Generally, we all know what emotions are. However, understanding how they affect us as leaders is different from defining them. There is a body of knowledge that has spread across the business landscape over several decades known as emotional intelligence. Much of what I have learned about emotional intelligence comes from the writings of Daniel Goleman, a well-known author, psychologist, and science journalist. In 1995, Goleman published his international best seller—*Emotional Intelligence*. In his book, Goleman defines emotional intelligence as "The capacity for recognizing our own feelings and those of others, for motivating ourselves, for managing emotions well in ourselves and in our relationships."[17]

Basically, if you understand your own emotional intelligence, you can use this knowledge to enhance it. More importantly, you can use your emotional intelligence to help manage your emotions better for the benefit of you and those around you. No matter how in control we are, at times we let our emotions interfere with the successful accomplishment of the tasks set before us. If we are aware of our own emotional strengths and weaknesses, we can manage our emotions appropriately.

Emotional intelligence is unique in itself and should not be confused with other categories of intelligence, e.g., technical and cognitive intelligence.[18] When you develop and use technical intelligence, you show that you understand the technical or functional aspects of something—let's say your job. If you are an accountant, your technical intelligence relates to the knowledge you have about accounting, internal controls, financial statement preparation, etc. If you are a purchasing agent, it includes your knowledge of the vendor selection process, contracts, bidding, vendor management, etc.

Your cognitive (or sometimes referred to as practical) intelligence is used to provide logic and reason in your thinking. It is the ability to read and write with understanding and coherence. It is the intelligence you use to analyze and prioritize things. I also consider "street smarts" as a part of cognitive intelligence. Cognitive intelligence is what you use to draw conclusions about the technical intelligence you have. An accountant assembles financial statement data and applies cognitive intelligence to understand the picture that the assembled data represents—e.g., our profits are increasing so we can invest in new services or marketplaces.

Many people are successful in the workplace by building these two intelligence capabilities alone without ever focusing on the third category—emotional intelligence. Remember, emotional intelligence is defined as "The capacity for recognizing our own feelings and those of others, for motivating ourselves, for managing emotions well in ourselves and in our relationships." So while you can be successful in your job using both technical and cognitive intelligence, you will be more effective when you also employ emotional intelligence in your role as a leader.

Failure to understand and manage one's own emotions often contributes to failure as a leader. In fact, did you know that one of the most frequently cited reasons for someone being fired is due to their inability to behave well in relationships with others—individually or in teams? Generally, people are not let go because they are technically incompetent or because they have low cognitive intelligence. Instead, most terminations revolve around behavioral issues. Many of these behavioral issues relate to weaknesses in emotional intelligence. With respect to leadership, many surveys indicate that employees leave their companies because of the weak or poor emotional intelligence and behavior of their leaders.

Think for a minute about your current employment. Are you comfortable with your own technical and cognitive intelligence? How do you feel about your own emotional intelligence? Is the idea of emotional intelligence and its impact on your success a new topic for you? If so, what can you do about it? How can you learn more about your emotional intelligence, measure your competencies, and more productively manage these behaviors?

If you are curious about your emotional intelligence, start by checking with the Human Resources department in your company. See if they can provide you with an assessment of emotional intelligence. Take it and then review it with an authorized representative. If your company does not have access to such a tool or cannot recommend an appropriate source, there are numerous leadership and coaching companies, individual executive coaches, psychiatrists, psychologists, and counselors who are trained administrators and interpreters to help you. You can also find suggested resources on Daniel Goleman's website at www. danielgoleman.info. I strongly encourage you to invest time learning more about your emotional intelligence. You cannot control the emotions and attitudes of those around you, but you can empower yourself with the knowledge you need to better manage your own emotional intelligence.

You can use what you learn about your own emotional intelligence to help you manage your emotions more effectively. I believe the best way to do that is to work with someone who is trained in helping people do so. Foremost, I believe the most important point to remember is this - you can only manage your own emotions. You cannot and should not try to manage others'. This is not a complicated thought. Yet, so often we try, by our words or actions, to control the emotions of those around us. Instead of worrying about others, we should be devoting our energy to managing ourselves.

Emotions themselves are not bad. Yes, there are emotions we label as bad and there are emotions we label as good. But bad emotions are not always bad, and good emotions are not always good. Instead, it is how you manage these emotions that will result in positive or negative actions arising from them.

The subjective nature of emotions makes it difficult to assess the cost of poor emotional intelligence or failure to manage emotions effectively. Studies demonstrate that the cost of poor emotional intelligence in the workplace can be significant. I'm sure we can all agree that we are not nearly as effective in our jobs or elsewhere when our emotions are out of control or are poorly managed.

Attitude

As I stated earlier in the chapter, I believe that our emotions are related to our attitude. So let me ask you. Do you have a good attitude or a bad attitude? What would your peers say about your attitude? Your boss? What would your family say?

When you were growing up, did you ever hear your parents say something like "You better change that attitude, young lady (or young man)"? Why is that? Do you remember how you responded? Did your attitude change in any dramatic way based on the feedback someone was giving you?

Attitudes, like emotions, affect us every day. Our own attitude, as well as the attitudes of those around us, have an impact on our daily lives. But who is in control of your attitude? Do you control your own attitude or do those around you control it?

Similarly to how I feel about emotions, I believe that no one can change your attitude but you. It is yours and yours alone to manage, to control, to shape. But just how easy is that to do?

Merriam-Webster defines attitude as, "A mental position with regard to a fact or state; a feeling or emotion toward a fact or state."[19]

Notice that the word *emotion* is included in the definition of attitude. Your attitude about a particular person, event, place, or thing is formed by events that have occurred and by the emotions resulting from those events. So, can you manage your attitude without managing your emotions? Let's take a look.

Here's an example: I don't like bees. Why? What is my reason? Well, when I was younger, I had a negative experience with bumblebees. So, even today, when I see one close by, I experience a fearful emotion. When I think or talk about bumblebees, it is obvious that my attitude toward them is less than favorable. My previous experience with bees has a direct impact on my current attitude.

An integral part of shaping our attitude is based on the emotions we experience. Emotions affect both our personal and professional lives. Sometimes we have them in control; sometimes, we don't. We experience emotions as high or low, positive or negative.

A colleague with significant experience in the leadership development field taught me a particular idea that to this day, resonates with me. Founder and CEO of Focus3, Tim Kight shared with me a straightforward technique to help manage my emotions. Since I learned it from him, I have adapted it to my own style and practiced it with some success. I believe you too can use it to manage your emotions and affect your attitudes about different things. Here's how I use it.

Think for a minute about an event, any event, bad or good, that has occurred. At the moment the event occurs, your mind tells you a story. This story in turn generates a feeling or emotion. The feeling or emotion begets a reaction. It is your reaction to this story that will ultimately affect your attitude. This process happens in a split second and feels like an almost-automatic response to the event you are experiencing.

Let me give you an example. Chad and Albert work together. Albert is Chad's boss, and he designated Chad as the project leader for a major client proposal. Chad has been hard at work for several weeks developing the proposal for delivery to the customer. It is now Friday afternoon, and the team is set to meet with the customer and deliver the proposal the following Thursday. Chad gave Albert a draft of the proposal on Monday, and asked him to provide review comments by Wednesday at 5:00 p.m. Chad is still waiting for Albert's comments.

At 3:30 p.m. on Friday, Albert walks into Chad's office and declares: "Chad, I have some issues with the proposal draft you gave me. There are some serious holes in it, and I need you to review my notes and make the necessary changes. I am leaving now for the weekend, but I need those edits completed by Monday morning. The customer called earlier this week to let me know they need to push up the meeting date due to a problem at one of their plants in South America. They'll be leaving on Tuesday morning, so we are meeting with the customer at 10:00 a.m. on Monday to review it. As such, we need to get together at 7:00 a.m. to finalize the proposal. If you have to call any of your staff in over the weekend to help you fix this thing, feel free to do so. We need to pull out all the stops on this one."

The event itself has occurred and now Chad's mind immediately begins telling him stories: "I can't believe I let Albert do this to me again! Here we are, down to the wire, and he comes in with all of these last minute changes and new information! When I gave him my proposal draft, I specifically told him I needed his comments by Wednesday afternoon. If he would have given them to me when I asked, I could have reviewed them with our staff, made the necessary changes, and been ready for an earlier meeting with the client. Now, I have to call them all and ruin their weekends by bringing them in on Saturday, and possibly Sunday, to work on this. They have seen this happen to our department before, and they are going to think I am a real jerk for letting it happen again! I am so mad at Albert, I could scream!"

"On top of that, Melanie is going to kill me. We made plans for a short getaway weekend beginning tonight. She has been working hard in her own job and cleared the weekend on her calendar. We were going to take off for one of her favorite resorts, have a couple of rounds of golf together, maybe hit the spa, and enjoy some nice, quiet evening dinners. Her mom and dad were looking forward to watching the kids, and now they will be disappointed too! Melanie is going to lay into me! I can hear her now! 'You let Albert do this to you all the time. He has behaved like this so many times before, and you just roll over and take it! Now we have to give up our weekend plans to appease him! On top of that, my mom and dad were so looking forward to watching the children! I can't believe you let this happen—again!'"

By now, what feelings are coursing through Chad's body? How has this event affected his attitude toward Albert, toward the project, even toward his job? What actions will he take as a result of the feelings coming from his mind's stories? Will he scream at Albert? Will he suppress his screams at Albert, but take it out on the other drivers on his way home? Or worse, will he dump on his wife and kids when he walks in the door?

Right now, Chad's emotions are strongly negative. His reaction to these feelings will also, most likely, be negative. How Chad handles his emotions at this time will directly impact his attitude. Chad's emotions will be affected by the stories his mind tells him based on this event. And how do you suppose this will affect his attitude towards Albert? His attitude towards Albert, and perhaps even the client, is not great. This negative attitude can carry forward in future relationships with Albert, or even have a secondary impact on the client relationship.

Think about your response in this situation. Would you have a choice in how you respond or would you blame Albert for your reaction? Would Albert's behavior cause your bad attitude? Your bad day? Your ruined weekend? Let's take a look at another way this could have gone.

Let's say the same facts take place, only when Albert lays all of this at Chad's feet, the stories in his mind go something like this: "I knew this would happen. This is classic Albert behavior. He has done this before. Well, it's a good thing I alerted the staff a couple of days ago to the idea that we may have to work this weekend. I told them not to make plans for the weekend; there was no way to be sure we would have it free.

I'm also glad that I alerted Melanie to the same possibility. Because this type of thing has happened before, we had backups for the plans we made this weekend. When I made our reservations at the resort, I checked on possible alternate dates. I also told her mom and dad that even if we have to cancel our plans, they can still take the kids. I would probably be working all day anyway. So, as much as I hate making all of these changes, it's not as bad as it could have been. Now, let me look at Albert's comments on the proposal and see how bad things really are."

In the second scenario, while the general outcome of the situation will not change, Chad's overall attitude will be more positive—or at least less negative and more productive. His reaction to Albert's last-minute antics will result in less anger and personal frustration.

Remember, the event itself didn't affect Chad's attitude. In fact, events don't shape attitudes at all. Contrary to what many of us believe, events don't cause us to have positive or negative emotions, nor do they cause us to have positive or negative attitudes about future events. Instead, we shape our own attitude based on how we manage or fail to manage our emotions. If we can learn to control our mental flow—from stories to feelings to reaction—we will be more in control of our emotions. If we manage our emotions to yield more positive results, we will have a different, more positive attitude.

So how do we do this? How do we adjust or control our mental flow? Let's go back to the beginning. An event takes place. Almost immediately, and without conscious thought, your brain starts working in overdrive, and your mind begins telling you stories. Right or wrong, fact or fiction, these stories rush through your mind. As a result, feelings or emotions are aroused. You experience physical reactions as emotions rush through your body—your fists clench, your stomach tightens up, you begin to sweat, you breathe more rapidly, your heart beats faster. You take action—you pound something, throw something, or scream at someone or something. An event occurs, stories rush in, feelings take over and action takes place. And, over time, your attitude about similar events is formed.

Because this process takes place so quickly, I believe you have to try and slow it down. Do something—take a deep breath, try to relax in some way—to absorb the event before your mind starts telling or repeating stories. Break it down and attempt to deal with it differently. Generate stories that help minimize the emotional damage.

Great advice, right? I agree that it is not easy to implement. In the moment, I find it almost impossible to slow things down. But as I understood this simple process, I began to force myself to more closely analyze the relationship of different types of events that trigger certain types of stories within me. As I looked back on them, I could understand the stories that my mind told me when the event occurred. I could also trace the impact of those stories on my feelings and actions. And I could understand how my emotions related to those events shaped my attitude toward similar events in the future. I have found that with recognition, analysis, and practice, I can discipline myself to control the stories and make them more positive. Or, at least I can make them less negative. This helps me maintain a better attitude and yields more positive actions overall.

When I think about the stories I tell myself and how they affect my emotions, I recall many instances in which I had thoughts like "George made me so mad the other day," or "I hate when he does that; he just makes me so angry when he does," or "I am so stupid! I could have seen this coming and I didn't! When will I ever learn?" I now know I have to slow down my thinking, try to cast out the bad stories, and bring in some good ones. It doesn't always work, but with recognition and practice it is easier to do. The bottom line is to recognize that no one else makes me mad. I let others make me angry; no one else arouses my emotions. I give them permission to make me angry by the stories I tell myself when these events occur. I have to slow down my thinking and break it down into manageable pieces. Doing so allows me to better manage my emotions.

As I work to manage my emotions, this technique has been helpful to me. It's a simple one to understand: event—story—feelings/emotions—action. And, it happens in a nanosecond. The brain is working at light speed reviewing stories about similar events in the past. We react to the stories with feelings and/or emotions that build within us, and then we take action. So we have to try to slow the process down. In some situations, I agree that is almost impossible to do. But we can take some time later to analyze what happened.

Think back to my story about the bumblebees. The event occurs—I am out for a walk around the neighborhood and see a bumblebee flying over a patch of flowers nearby. The stories flood my mind—you have been stung before; it is painful; bees are not your friend. The emotion that arises—fear. The action I take—walk away from the flowers faster.

Now let's say I am a beekeeper. The same event occurs, but the stories are different—bees are productive; they contribute to the environment; they make a great product. The resulting emotions—warmth and friendliness. The action—walk over and see if there is anything unique about this one, or look around to see if there are others operating in the area. Enjoy the bees and the flowers!

The attitude towards the bees is shaped by the emotional reactions of past experiences. Feelings about and attitude towards bees are perpetuated by the stories told when the event occurs. If you can control the stories your mind tells you, you can ultimately control your resulting emotions and attitude.

As I conclude this chapter, I want to share with you a story I have heard several times. It has slight variations, but pretty much goes like this:

An elderly grandfather of a Native American tribe was counseling his grandson about self-control. The grandfather tells his grandson, "Sometimes I feel as if I have two wolves fighting inside me. One is an evil, mangy-looking, growling wolf. The other is a good, beautiful, docile wolf. The evil wolf is angry and violent; the good wolf is full of love and compassion." When the grandson asks the grandfather which wolf will win the fight, the grandfather simply says, "The one I feed."[20]

Remember, you are in control. You can control your emotions, and ultimately, your attitude. The stories you tell yourself when an event occurs are the logs you throw on your emotional fire. They are the food you feed the wolves inside you. Fire can be good or it can be harmful. What kind of emotional fire will you choose to burn? Which wolf will you feed? The choice is yours. But remember, your choice will determine your outcome.

CHAPTER 11

———

ETHICS

Ethics. Such a small word that can mean so much and cause so much consternation. When I first decided to write a chapter on ethics, I struggled with what to say. After all, some of the world's greatest, most well-known men and women—philosophers, scientists, moralists, authors, educators, religionists—from all walks of life, have wrestled with the subject. Why would I think that I could explain it better than them?

As I began to frame my point of view though, I realized I do not need to go back to Socrates or Plato or Aristotle or Aquinas, to cite my observations about the subject. And after all, that's what this book is—my observations, my beliefs.

A simple oft-quoted thought to describe ethical behavior says: "Do unto others as you would have them do to you."[21] Most of you know these words from the Bible—either Luke 6:31 (New International Version) (www.biblegateway.com) or Matthew 7:12. But you might be a bit surprised to learn that this thought is not just the province of Christendom. According to Wikipedia (http://en.wikipedia.org/wiki/Golden_Rule), you find similar references to it throughout the world in different religions.

For a topic that has been around so long, why do most of us find it difficult to define? If someone were to ask you for a definition, what would you say? How would you define ethics? Do you consider yourself an ethical person? Do others think you are an ethical person? Who is the most ethical person you know?

As part of my coaching work, I often converse with clients and others about what is the "right thing to do." I am more than happy to have those discussions, but in my role as a coach, in fact, in my role as a fellow human being, it is not my place to tell others how to behave ethically. Each one of us must choose for ourselves what that means. And although I will not tell someone how to behave ethically, I am willing to share my own thoughts on the subject.

But first, we must define ethics. According to Dictionary.com, ethics is defined as:

ethics [eth-iks] - plural noun
1. (used with a singular or plural verb) a system of moral principles: (the ethics of a culture).

2. the rules of conduct recognized in respect to a particular class of human actions or a particular group, culture, etc.: (medical ethics; Christian ethics).

3. moral principles, as of an individual: (His ethics forbade betrayal of a confidence).

4. (usually used with a singular verb) that branch of philosophy dealing with values relating to human conduct, with respect to the rightness and wrongness of certain actions and to the goodness and badness of the motives and ends of such actions.[22]

When discussing ethical behavior, I often frame my questions on this topic around the concept of trust. After all, if a person behaves in an ethical manner, it is more than likely that they can be trusted. While most people find it difficult to provide a specific definition of ethics, they are able to talk about trust. For example, instead of asking: "Is Bill ethical?" I will ask "What are the behaviors that Bill exhibits that support your trust in him?"

The answers I have received to these questions helped me to shape my own beliefs about what it means to behave ethically. My purpose in writing this chapter is not to tell you how to act. However, it is my hope that you find this list helpful as you assess the ethical behaviors of yourself and others, as you develop your own personal, ethical guidelines and as you strive to live your life ethically.

An individual that lives life ethically:

- **Always does what she says she will do.** If she makes a commitment, she will do everything she can to fulfill it.

- **Informs others if he is unable to meet his commitment.** If circumstances change, he will let someone know as soon as he can that he can no longer live up to the established expectations.

- **Keeps confidences.** He does not share specific issues about professional or personal life. If she feels that it becomes necessary for her to do so, she asks permission to share information. In addition, he does not share items that he has learned in confidence from others. When specifically asked about an individual's behavior, he politely refuses to discuss it if it was told to him in confidence.

- **Walks her talk.** Her behavior is consistent with the way she talks about doing things and the way she believes that others should behave in specific circumstances. She conducts her life consistently with her beliefs and values.

- **Holds himself accountable.** If he is not able to do what was promised, he informs the appropriate parties. He takes responsibility for his actions. If something goes wrong, he does not point the finger or blame others. He carefully evaluates what happened, fairly states the facts, and bears his share of the responsibility.

- **Is committed to doing the right thing.** She doesn't just react to situations. She thinks things through carefully when faced with a difficult decision.

- **Compromises.** No matter what the issue or problem is, he recognizes and values the input and suggestions of others, but does not compromise his principles.

- **Builds arguments and positions based on facts – not rumor or the opinions of others.** But she will consider the opinions of others as she interprets the facts. She thinks straight.

- **Tells it like he sees it.** He doesn't pull any punches. He is open in his communications. When necessary, and out of respect for other parties in the conversation, he tempers his directness in an appropriate manner. But he still makes his point. He talks straight.

- **Sets high standards and holds herself accountable.** She sets clear expectations and expects others to hold themselves accountable.

- **Treats others with dignity and respect and expects others to do the same.** She interacts in a positive way with colleagues that demonstrates her regard for them, practices treating those around her with integrity, and holds her peers to the same standard.

- **Asks nicely.** She always asks and encourages; she doesn't demand. However, as mentioned earlier, she will not compromise on a matter of her own principles. She will state her position firmly. And when finished, she says thank you.

I think it's easy to describe how you act "ethically." You do it with truth, dignity, respect, accountability, appreciation, gratitude, commitment, consistency—there are many words you can use to describe trust, to describe ethical behavior. But while it may be easy to describe how to act ethically, it is not always easy to do so. There can be tremendous pressure on you—outside pressures or self-imposed pressures—to act in a manner that is inconsistent with your own ethical beliefs. And I offer no magic solution, no get-out-of-jail-free card, to help you decide how to behave in such circumstances. I do recommend you follow the first phrase in my book title—Think Straight:

- Understand all of the facts about your situation and the potential ramifications of it. Do as much research as you feel necessary to obtain the relevant facts.

- Understand your own morals, your own values, your own beliefs. Consider the philosophical, religious, legal, etc. guidance that is available to you in doing so.

- Weigh the facts as you understand them against your principles, act accordingly and take responsibility for your actions.

- And beyond the individual situations, establish your own ethical beliefs in your own simple rules of life, in your own words. Feel free to use the words of another, if you feel they state it better. Keep these words close to you and revisit them often.

After you think straight, then talk straight. And walk your talk.

Every day we are faced with decisions that require us to decide how we will act. Will we choose to act ethically or unethically? Unfortunately, there will always be temptations to choose unethical behavior. If you don't believe me, look at the many examples in the world around you of unethical decisions. However, you don't have to be like others around you. You can choose to live your life ethically. It will take effort as you strive to maintain your core values and act accordingly, but remember, you are the one who has to live with your decisions.

CHAPTER 12

———

CULTURE

In the next chapter, we will discuss the concept of networking and I will share some of my thoughts on how to network effectively. However, just because you know how to network, doesn't mean you will choose to join a particular network, right? What is it about a specific network that makes you want to be a part of it? For that matter, the same question should be asked about any company you work for or any organization you are a member of.

In most situations, you will join a company, organization, or network because its culture is something you believe in; it motivates or inspires you. You want to be a part of it.

I can best address my thoughts about culture, in any organization or network, by telling you my own story about the organizational culture that I have valued the most throughout my career. It is also the culture by which I measure all other network and organizational cultures. It is the culture I was first exposed to over 40 years ago and even though the business no longer exists, I am still actively involved in the network that carries on that culture.

I was with Arthur Andersen for over 30 years and the impact it had on me was significant. In 2002, the firm stopped operating and I began a new career. However, there are clusters of Arthur Andersen alumni around the world who still get together to share their experiences and maintain a level of camaraderie that you don't often see in existing organizations today. So why is it that this network is very much alive yet other networks I have joined over the years have lost their luster? What is different about this particular network and what is it about the connections that we have to a nonexistent organization that keeps us coming back together?

While the network has value to all of us, we remain connected because of the culture that attracted us and still appeals and serves today. These cultural ties are apparent all over the world as evidenced by a volunteer-led and distributed quarterly newsletter to thousands of alums, numerous events that groups of Arthur Andersen alumni organized around the globe, consistent connections through links provided by social media sites, and the formation of businesses that reflect similar cultures in their operations today.

As John Donne, an English poet, said: "No man is an island..."[23] We are interdependent beings. There are very few hermits in this world, and even they occasionally interact with others. If we are to have the kind of life we desire, we have to work and play in the sandbox with others. The groups with whom we associate are our networks. The culture of those networks is what keeps us together. The stronger the culture, the stronger the network. A strong culture benefits an organization or a network by serving as the glue that holds it together. I have heard one leadership guru say that culture is what takes place when no one is watching. Because culture is personal to each of us, I don't know that I can specifically define what a good culture is for you, but I know what a good culture is for me when I see it.

I believe a beneficial culture is one that honors people—whether they are employees, customers, suppliers, or other stakeholders. It is the culture of the company to treat everyone with respect. It is one that creates an environment in which everyone can grow based on their performance. It doesn't take advantage of anyone; it treats people fairly. It is an organization that is committed to the concept of stewardship—the belief that all members of the culture have the responsibility to continue to build a better environment for those who follow. (I will talk about this more in a later chapter.) My "best culture" organization communicates regularly with me. It informs me of both good and bad news. It helps me align my expectations for growth with the organization's growth and it creates an environment that allows me to grow as much as I can. The culture and the people involved hold me accountable and demand that I do so of myself and others. This culture is also interested in my continued development and challenges me to continue to grow.

These are elements I look for in a culture. As you plan your life and career, growth and development, and goals for success, you should outline your own elements of a good culture and seek out organizations that possess them. This is an idea that is sometimes overlooked when we are looking for a job or networks to join.

The culture of a company permeates the organization—whether it is a formally structured one or an informal network. It is the glue that keeps the organization together. If the culture is good, it has positive benefits to its members. If the culture is negative, it will infect and often break down the network. I believe Arthur Andersen had a very positive culture. It was one that we all wanted to be a part of and still want to be a part of to this day.

Organizational culture should be supportive, dependable, and educational. When each member of an organization believes in its culture, their behavior is consistent with its values and the organization operates more smoothly. For example, a community-based network providing services to children in need will be populated with members who want to meet that goal. Individuals whose behaviors are inconsistent with that of the culture will be forced out. If a company has a strong culture of delivering the highest quality of customer service, sales personnel who don't support this concept will have limited careers. The existing sales ecosystem will force them out.

But just as positive cultures will propel a network, a negative one will break it down. There are no benefits to being involved in a network or organization that has a poor culture. In fact, it can be detrimental to your success. If you do not believe you are in a positive culture, it is time to find a new job, network, or organization.

I am not an anthropologist and have certainly not studied cultures in depth. I have, however, learned certain attributes of a culture that are important and that build value. I do not expect that you would adopt my cultural beliefs, but I do believe you should give some periodic and regular thought to the culture of your own organizations and networks. What is important to you that impels you to be in a network with others?

What follows in this chapter is a list of elements of the culture I experienced at Arthur Andersen. I look for these in other organizations I frequent and I try to model them in my own life. I share these with you to expand upon the comments I made earlier about the benefits of a culture. These culture elements are the ones most relevant to me. They are offered to provoke your own thinking about the type of culture you would prefer in the networks in which you participate. You have to think about your own value system, your own ethics and beliefs. Then create your own list of cultural elements that you look for in your networks, companies, and organizations.

Think Straight. Talk Straight. As I have mentioned in the earlier chapter of the same name and throughout many other chapters, Arthur Andersen himself was quoted as saying that this belief never failed him. Ever since I heard it on my first day of employment with Arthur Andersen, it never failed me either. It resonates deeply with me in both my personal life and in my professional life. I value its meaning, and if it resonates with you, I hope it is part of your culture.

Keep it simple. Throughout all stages of my career, I was taught to strive to reduce the complexities of my profession—accounting and auditing—to simple statements and explanations. The simplest one is "The debits must always equal the credits." It can take some complicated analysis to show others this accounting truism, but once the analysis is complete, the answer is usually pretty simple and uncomplicated. In fact, this simple accounting theorem can be taken into all phases of life. If things are out of balance, eventually, something goes wrong. Don't over-complicate things. Life can be complicated enough. Strive to build a culture free of complexities.

Invest in your people. Any organization, public or private, has one singular most important asset—its people. It can have the best software in the world; it can have the best weaponry in a war; the best pizza in the city; the best automobile on the road. But none of these things, none of its services are invented, manufactured, designed, or delivered without people.

The most successful organizations—the ones who are regularly named "the best to work for"—make a significant commitment to their people. At Arthur Andersen, every individual, regardless of title or position was exposed to the culture, processes, and organization from the moment they were hired. Every one of us who joined the organization over the years attended an initial firm-wide staff training school. Throughout the world, these classes were often held at a campus-like facility in which people lived together for a number of days or even weeks. Various levels of this training were continually presented to us throughout our careers—even at the most senior levels. A majority of our training contributed to our growth in the technical side of our professions (accounting, auditing, tax, consulting, technology, etc.). But there was also a significant amount of training geared toward developing us as managers and leaders of people. This behavioral training included public speaking, business writing, selling professional services, teamwork, diversity, ethics, and many others. Opportunities also existed to study and learn outside the organization through participation in professional or trade organizations.

I remember really feeling the power of our commitment to train and invest in our people when I was first asked to serve as an instructor in one of the training schools. The amount of support given to me as an instructor was tremendous. It helped me prepare for and successfully deliver that program and many others over the years.

In addition to its commitment to its people through professional training and development, Arthur Andersen had coaching, mentoring and other similar programs available to help employees navigate their way to a successful career.

Another important aspect about this "commitment to people" is that it does not just apply to those who are engaged in the primary production or output of the organization. It applies to administrators, technologists, and other professional support staff. If a business states that it "invests in its people," there has to be evidence that this investment occurs across the board for all members of the organization.

While I am singularly proud of the investment in people that our firm made, I have since learned of many other organizations that make a similar commitment to their people. If you belong to an organization that does invest in its people, I hope you are taking advantage of your company's commitment. If your organization does not make this commitment to its people, I challenge you to think about how important this is to your self-development and to do something about it.

Commit to quality. Whether your business produces a product or a service, it is critical that quality be a primary deliverable. In our services firm, if you had to deal with a difficult accounting or tax issue, or if you had a client that wanted to significantly deviate from an established principle or methodology, there was a thorough process you had to follow to resolve the situation. Similarly, I focus my purchase of products and services for my own purposes on organizations that provide top quality. I don't believe any organization can survive very long if it doesn't have commitment to quality of service or product as a major tenet of its culture.

Provide excellent service. From the day I joined Arthur Andersen and attended our firm-wide training school, it was clear to me that our primary mission was to deliver quality client service. Every employee was committed to making sure that the service we delivered met or exceeded the client's expectations. I witnessed people jump on planes, trains, and automobiles to meet a client requirement—often at the drop of a hat. Employees made business and personal sacrifices to deliver the best service possible. Yet, when a client's demands were excessive or inappropriate, the firm was also willing to tell the client "No" instead of sacrificing its integrity or beliefs.

Be a good steward. The concept of stewardship was introduced to me during my initial employment interview when I was still on campus. A partner told me that it was his responsibility to " . . . make this a better place for the people that follow me . . . because those ahead of me made it a great place for me." That concept resonated with me. I found myself repeating it often to others throughout my career. I think it is a principle all of us can follow in both our business and personal lives.

Top-notch organizations not only expect their successful people to be good stewards of the organizations, but also good stewards of the industry or the profession in which they work and compete. These businesses support their peoples' participation in trade organizations and professional associations. Some of their employees become recognized experts in their profession or industry by serving in leadership roles on committees, task forces, and other groups. Good companies in specific industries have key personnel in significant knowledge roles. Look around inside good businesses and you will find positions occupied by persons who are considered the best electrical engineer, or the best hospital administrator, or the highest caliber research scientist. In addition to providing deep technical knowledge within the company, these employees are also encouraged by their businesses to participate in selected industry groups. These organizations recognize the importance of contributing to industry growth and direction. By helping their employees become good stewards beyond the company, they publicly support such growth.

In the best of companies, this commitment of stewardship also extends to the community. Companies encourage their executives to serve on the boards of community organizations. They promote volunteer activity within their employee base by creating activities such as service days or community commitment days. In these activities, employees are granted a certain amount of company time to share their skills and abilities with others in order to build a home for homeless people, paint a school, or help an organization develop its supply chain. I have seen numerous examples of these community partnerships throughout my business career and I hope you have the opportunity to work in an organization that promotes this type of stewardship. It is not only good for you and the company, but for the community as well.

Have a unifying concept. In the early 70s, I had my first opportunity to travel to several international offices in the firm. I was the audit manager on a major client with locations around the world. Until that first overseas trip, I was aware of what our company described as the "one-firm concept." I heard partners and managers talk about it often. The trip really brought the idea home to me. I reviewed dozens of work paper files that were prepared consistently with the format and processes I was familiar with back home. I met dozens of staff, managers and partners who spoke of the firm, its policies, its practices, and its culture, in the same way I did. Many of them even had some of the same complaints! It was a down-to-earth demonstration of a principle that I heard many times. I finally appreciated its effectiveness. No matter what country we operated in, no matter the common language or customs of the local offices, we were one organization. We were built around a consistent culture, had a consistent vision and applied consistent processes and principles to achieve them. We viewed our service requirements as meeting the same or higher principles than our profession's standards. We felt it was necessary to maintain these principles in order to deliver excellent service of the highest quality. Yes, we adapted them for local cultural differences, but we stuck to them. If you give some thought to it, I know you can think of other business organizations who reflect this concept of "one organization" devoted to the same principles and values across the globe.

This same concept holds true regardless of the size of your organization or your team. Regardless of where you are trying to build your culture, a unifying concept will not only simplify processes, but help foster a feeling of unity.

Build your own networks. A quality company with a good culture en-courages its employees to build and travel within their own networks. There are networks all around us that promote professional skills, spe-cific industries or professions, and personal skills development. Find the ones that fit your development and participate in them. As I grew throughout my career, my firm encouraged and supported my network development in a variety of ways. What are the networks in which you participate? Are they college alumni clubs, professional associations, trade or business groups, religious institutions, community, or social not-for-profit organizations? Does your company promote your in-volvement in them? If so, in what ways? If not, why not?

Honor alumni. I opened this chapter by relating my experience as an alum of Arthur Andersen. I often hear someone tell a story of a suc-cessful opportunity that came through our alumni relationships—and not just increased business or other monetary opportunities. Any good organization recognizes the value that exists in its former employees— its alumni. Some companies include them in their current activities. Many businesses regularly communicate with its population of former employees. However it's accomplished, I believe it is important to keep those lines of communications open, to keep those relationships flour-ishing.

Be consistent. I have occasionally heard others (including myself) joke that, "Consistency is the standard of the unimaginative." Taken to the greatest degree, this may be true as it can mean reluctance or refusal to change. But I hope you see throughout the points I outlined as good for a culture, that consistency must exist in order for the organization and everyone in it to be efficient, effective, and productive. Consisten-cy also applies to change. You have to be consistently on the alert to recognize the need to change and have a consistent process to imple-ment change throughout the organization. And you need a consistent process to recognize when change is not the right thing to do.

A good culture attracts you, recharges you, and maintains you. Unfor-tunately, I don't think most of us give much thought to the subject of culture, especially as it relates to work. I think each of us should give more thought to it which is why I wrote this chapter. I hope this chap-ter provokes your thinking about culture. I believe these are aspects of a great culture and that a great culture is something everyone should experience. Even after Arthur Andersen disappeared, I continue to support and utilize the aspects of culture I learned decades ago. These cultural features I enumerated need not be yours. However, you should know what you want in a culture and you should put forth the energy to seek it out. You should want to be a part of the culture of any organization (business, civic, community, professional or social network, etc.) you join. As another colleague in the leadership business once shared, you should own your own part of the organization's culture.

I believe in a positive culture that attracts positive people who want to do positive things. I believe in a culture that values paying it forward. I want to belong to businesses, organizations, and networks that reflect this positivity.

So ask yourself, what values are there in your networks, your organizations? What is their culture? What is the culture you are looking for? How do you contribute to those values and help sustain the culture? I challenge you to understand your own values, and measure them against the culture of the organizations in which you live and work. Are they consistent? If so, challenge yourself to continue to build and promote that culture. It is truly a rewarding feeling that I hope you can experience in your career and your life. If the organization or network culture is not consistent with your own, you have a choice. Modify your own values or change the organizations or networks in which you associate.

Over the years, I have been asked if I understood and appreciated the value of the culture at Arthur Andersen during my tenure there, or if I wasn't able to appreciate its full value until I had moved onto the next phase of my life. Honestly, I am still unsure. What I do know is that I did not want to leave the culture at Arthur Andersen, and that I have missed it since leaving the company. The effects of the AA culture on my career and life are profound. To this day, I find myself trying to live out that culture in my daily life. It is my hope that as you move through your career and life that you may find a culture you feel as passionately about as I do about Arthur Andersen. You deserve to experience the positive influence that a company's culture can have, for its effects can last a lifetime.

CHAPTER 13

NETWORKING

Network. Network. Network!

How many times have you heard this advice before? Probably a lot! Nonetheless, knowing you should network and actually networking are two totally different things. Networking takes time and the rewards are rarely instantaneous. However, when done correctly, networking can have huge payoffs for your job and your career.

There are many formal definitions of networking; here are three:

- The exchange of information or services among individuals, groups, or institutions; the cultivation of productive relationships for employment or business.[24]

- The act of meeting new people in a business context.[25]

- A supportive system of sharing information and services among individuals and groups having a common interest.[26]

Here is my straightforward and simple definition: **Networking is purposefully connecting with people.**

There are many different avenues for networking. Networking can be done face-to-face or over the phone. It can be done via email, Twitter, or other social media sites. Call me old-fashioned, but my preference is still to network face-to-face. While there is value in virtual networking, face-to-face conversations are still the richest form of communication. Face-to-face networking allows a more personal connection to be made. Personal connections are often lost when we use technology as our networking platform. I hope that although you utilize technology for some of your networking needs, you never lose the desire or the ability to communicate face-to-face. As with any skill, the less you use it, the faster you will lose it. Be sure to maintain a balance between virtual and face-to-face networking. Since my passion lies with face-to-face networking, and it is often the most challenging form for most people, that will be the focus in this chapter.

Networking takes place for a variety of different reasons. However, our own needs should never be the primary driver for networking. First and foremost, service to others should be our primary consideration when networking. Practically, I don't expect everyone to think, "I am going to go to that association meeting tonight to help others deal with their problems." But, as you do meet with individuals, I encourage you to have thoughts like, "What has he been dealing with that I can offer some suggestions about?" or "What problem is she facing that I can help her with—either from my own background or by suggesting they connect with someone else?" You can even help by offering more personal suggestions, such as recommending a particular movie or book you recently enjoyed.

Networking feels better, and very often more natural, when we think about helping others. When we take the focus off our own needs and direct it towards helping someone else, we are more comfortable in our approach and typically more successful. But, of course, realistically speaking we also network for our own purposes. We attend a professional association meeting to expand our professional relationships or our business knowledge. We go to a favorite club to seek out social relationships. We network to learn about new organizations. When we are in a career or job transition, we network to meet people who can help us with our search—by sharing ideas with them, by sharing leads with them, by brainstorming potential contacts, and by securing informational interviews. We network to identify potential customers, to promote our products and services, and to identify potential people who can help us solve a problem. And although we network for a variety of reasons, we should always have the "end in mind" of helping those we meet in order to help ourselves. We should pay it forward.

One of the greatest challenges regarding networking is that it requires an investment of time. Through my own personal networks, I often meet many people who are in career transition. They will tell me that they have not maintained their networks while they have been in full-time work mode. Then, when the inevitable job change or restructuring occurs, they find themselves in startup networking mode all over again. In order to avoid this situation, it is essential that you discipline yourself to build your network in a way that flexes with your needs over time, but does not completely dissipate. Naturally, you will network more when you are going through job or career transition. But don't let that be the only networking you do.

For example, as I moved into the post-Andersen stage of my life, I took the time to identify certain groups I wished to use as my primary base for networking. Some were local and some were national in scope. When we decided to relocate from Chicago to Dallas, I had the opportunity to use the national network organizations as a starting point for building my network in Dallas. In addition, I sought out other new local groups. Now that we have been here for several years, I shuffle and reshuffle the groups that I frequent, depending on the business and other activities I have going on in my life. But, I don't let relations with any one group go unconnected for too long.

In order to keep networking present in your life, you may find it advantageous to set a goal for yourself on a weekly, monthly, or quarterly basis. Setting a goal will help ensure networking remains a focus even though it may not be your main priority. For example, a business group to which I belong has a monthly meeting—usually with a guest speaker or panel activity. I attend their meetings when I have an interest in the subject being presented. But at a minimum, I try to attend this group three or four times a year.

Once you agree that networking is important, what can you do to maximize the effectiveness of your networking efforts? Here are some ideas to consider.

Have a plan. Put some thoughts together on what you would like to accomplish for each networking group you plan to join. Consider the following in your plan:

- Gather background information on the nature of the group— what do they represent, why do they get together, who is most likely to attend?

- Try to obtain a list of attendees in advance and identify specific people you would like to meet.

- Summarize your objectives. What would you like to learn about or accomplish with the people you meet? Have two or three objectives in mind for each networking event (e.g., the number of new business cards you would like to collect; the number of follow-up appointments or phone call commitments you would like to make; a specific person or two that you would like to meet if you know they are attending, etc.). Remember, service to others should be your primary focus. If you are having a networking meeting or telephone conversation with one person, generate a list of key points that you wish to cover in the conversation. For example, I often suggest to those in transition to have a short list of companies or industries in which they have an interest. You can share this list and find out whether or not the person can help you make a connection.

Understand your personal behavior style. It is important to remember your primary behavioral preferences when you are networking. For example, if one of your primary behavioral preferences is extroversion, you might try to meet too many people at a networking event, and not focus sufficiently on a specific person or two with whom you would like to connect. Or, if your primary behavioral preference is introversion, you might limit your conversations to such brevity that you do not sufficiently make your point with others or gather the information you desire. Knowing your style will raise awareness for your preferred behaviors and hopefully help you modify your behavior accordingly.

Vary your questioning technique. Be specific and have a focus, but don't be so specific that you box out the potential answers of others by asking them strictly close-ended questions. Close-ended questions are an important part of a networking conversation when blended with open-ended ones. For example, assume you are networking during job transition. You are attending a meeting which might include people that work with or are familiar with one of your target companies. After breaking the ice and getting into the flow of the conversation, consider asking a blend of questions, such as:

- "Do you happen to know anyone who works in the engineering department at XYZ?" (Closed)

- "If not, how do you think I might connect with someone in the engineering department?" (Open)

- "Who else at XYZ do you think I might try to connect with?" (Closed)

- "There are several other businesses in our community that are similar to XYZ—such as ABC, 123, etc. Do you happen to know anyone who works at any one of these companies?" (Closed)

- "Given your understanding of my background, how would you go about identifying other companies or organizations similar to XYZ that I should consider in my search?" (Open)

Create your "elevator speech" and practice it. This is your commercial, the statement of your brand. It should be about 60-90 seconds long. No longer, no shorter. Divide up the content to give the listener approximately 1/3 about who you are, and 2/3 about what you can do for them or their organization.

Elevator speech
60 – 90 seconds

For example, "Hi. I'm Ed Maier and I am an executive coach. I have over forty years of business experience as an accounting and finance professional and a business leader. I use this experience, along with my coaching process, to help people improve their personal effectiveness and leadership skills—in such areas as communication and presentations, managing accountability of yourself and others, and building teamwork and collaboration—just to name a few."

We tend to think that we only need the elevator speech when we are networking for a job, or networking to sell something to another. But a good elevator speech is a great door-opener for any conversation with someone new. Used properly, an elevator speech is brief and to the point. It creates a launching pad for the conversation and invites the other party to join in the discussion. You will not spend your time talking on and on about yourself.

I have created and re-created elevator speeches for myself numerous times and you will too. It is important to create one that you are comfortable with and works well for you.

Practice great listening skills. Reframe comments others make or repeat them back in order to demonstrate you are listening. Work hard to have the other person talk more than you do. Ask questions to clarify points. Provide good feedback when necessary. Use each networking opportunity as a chance to learn. After each interaction you should be able to answer the question, "What did I learn about him/her that I did not know before?"

Practice networking. Networking comes more naturally to some of us than others. If networking pushes you outside of your comfort zone, remember to implement ideas that feel more natural to you and practice, practice, practice. But don't just practice your elevator speech and your listening skills. Practice networking so it appears more natural when you are engaged in an event.

Maintain good eye contact. Don't let your eyes wander around the room. Remember my story of being called on the carpet by a senior executive who believed I was not giving him my full attention in a networking conversation? Don't allow your roving eyes to deflect you from having a direct conversation with someone else. You owe them the respect of your undivided attention.

Know when to stop talking and when to leave the conversation. In some instances, you will want to shorten your conversation. Learn to gracefully exit a conversation when necessary so you don't just abruptly walk away. Other networkers understand that you will not be talking to them the entire length of the meeting. Just be courteous about how you end a conversation and move along. Leave the conversation gracefully and politely. But, do it firmly so that your listener doesn't end up "hanging on." For example, you might say something like: "I appreciate your thoughts. Thanks very much for your help. I am going to continue to circulate around the room and meet a few others. If you would like to discuss this in greater detail, perhaps we should set up a separate conversation. Would you like to meet over coffee some time?" I find that many of us are uncomfortable in breaking off a networking conversation. Personally, I believe the direct approach is the best. So, I like to thank people for their time and excuse myself to circulate the room and meet others. Generally, however, the separation occurs very naturally.

Follow up and follow through (or not). Many people do a great job at the conversational part of networking, but they don't follow through. Always follow-up on opportunities to connect with others. Leave the conversation by either making a commitment to follow-up with the other party, or asking them to follow-up with you. Also, recognize that you will not wish to follow-up with everyone you meet and that is okay. Since networking takes time, it is important to spend your follow up time wisely.

Dress appropriately. In my many years in business, I have seen a dramatic change in what is acceptable dress in the workplace. I accept the fact that standards have changed. Different businesses have different dress codes that fit their culture. If they are successful, who am I to challenge their policies? If possible, inquire about the dress code prior to the event. But when you go to a function outside of your company, if you cannot inquire about the dress code beforehand, I believe you should "dress up" more than you usually would. Strive to be dressed one level above the majority of the group. Call me old-fashioned, but business networking functions are no place for flip-flops, shorts, t-shirts, blue jeans with holes, and shoes that don't look like they have been cleaned or polished since the animals walked off the ark!

Exchange appropriate business information with the people you meet. Offer business cards or resumes. I cannot tell you how many times I hear people say "Oh, I forgot my business cards." First of all, this should be an exchange of information so be sure you get their information as well. When you get their information, you are in control of follow up instead of relying on them to make contact. When you return to your home or office, put them in your contact file. Send them an email with your contact information, and thank them for the conversation. Since I am forgetful, I try to minimize the risk of forgetting my business cards by making sure one pocket of every jacket I wear has a small supply of business cards. I keep mine in the left pocket; I put those I receive in the right pocket. For my female business friends, I suggest keeping a small supply of business cards in each purse you own. And, when you switch purses, just leave them in the purse you emptied. They will be there the next time you use it. In addition, you should always have some at random social events. I also keep a set in my car's glove compartment, in each briefcase or portfolio I use, and even in my golf bag!

Send a note. When you have a networking experience in which someone does something for you, connects you with someone else, or just takes the time to provide you with some good ideas, send them a timely thank-you note. I won't debate whether they should be text messages, emails, typed letters, or personal notes. Do whatever you prefer, whatever fits your personal style, and try to gear it toward their preferred method of contact. You may even ask them during your interaction, "What is your preferred method of contact?" And, always thank others for the help they give you.

Respond. We all know the Golden Rule or some version of it: "Do unto others as you would have them do unto you." When it comes to networking, I suggest you adopt your own Golden Rule: "Return the phone calls and email messages of others as you would have them return yours." If you leave a message and state that you would like a response, you should follow up with them until you get it. You should also respond to those who ask you for follow up. Even if it is to say, "No."

Develop a personal tracking method to monitor your networking activities. There are a variety of tools available to you: electronic spreadsheets, software programs, smart phone applications, business card storage containers, and even post-it notes. Develop and use a method that fits your style. Review your tracking system results periodically to maintain contact with people.

Follow up on your commitments; and don't be afraid to remind others about theirs. For certain, you want to make sure that you have your own system for following up on the commitments you make to others. When you keep network commitments, you demonstrate your accountability. And, if someone makes a commitment to do something for you, politely hold them to their commitment. If you have not heard back in a few days, follow up.

Frequently, I hear the question: "How often should I follow up with people who have said they will get back to me or introduce me to someone or provide additional information? I don't want them to think I am a pest!" If someone makes a commitment to you, direct or indirect, you should follow up with them until that commitment is resolved or accomplished. It is appropriate to reach out to someone periodically to remind them that you are waiting for their follow up. For example, if someone promises to send you a networking connection or introduce you to someone in their company, I recommend your first follow-up be no longer than two weeks out. Continue to follow up on a periodic basis (every two to four weeks) until they have responded. People get busy; people are forgetful. If you politely remind them of their commitment, most people usually respond and may even appreciate the reminder.

Stay in touch. I can't tell you how many times the following happens. I meet someone in career or job transition. We have a good discussion. I offer them some thoughts on their process or even make a few introductions for them. And I never hear from them again. As you do your own networking—whether it is for transition purposes or for creating opportunities to make sales calls—it is OK, and often appreciated, to periodically let others know how you are progressing. If you are in transition, develop a batch list of people with whom you have networked and occasionally (e.g., once a month, every other month, etc.) send out an email to remind people you are still in the market and what types of opportunities you are seeking. I have even seen some correspondences in which people mention the types of interviews they have recently had. If you are networking primarily in a sales-focused role, I think it is also important to maintain contact with your potential customer (e.g., remind them about your product or service, send them a recent product update, send a newsletter or business article you read in which they might have an interest, etc.). Creating such touch points in a positive, professional manner is well-regarded by most recipients.

Always be polite. Remember to say, "Please" and "Thank you." This seems like such a straightforward concept, but it is surprising how our behaviors can change when we get busy or stressed. Also, if someone gives you a positive response to one of your questions about which company or person to connect with, don't just say, "Thank you." Ask if they can provide you with an introduction, even if only by email. If they do not feel they can make an introduction, ask their thoughts on how you might reach out to your target.

Network with different groups (or start your own group). You don't just have to network with business groups all the time. Consider connecting with a group related to a hobby or an interest other than your career or profession. Think about the organizations in which you participate or the things you have in common with others. If networking is not a part of it, set up a network and see what happens. It can be a group of hobbyists; a group from one of your church's ministries; a book club;

fellow coaches in a youth soccer league; any organization that regularly gathers for a purpose also provides the opportunity for networking. For example: One of the volunteer organizations I work with recently established a program to connect individual members with each other to have coffee or lunch. The purpose is to help us get to know each other better. Remember, any business or organization that encourages "internal" networking helps build its culture. Another of my colleagues decided that a small circle of her business associates should get together occasionally to discuss common interests. She started with a small group and has now grown it to a larger one that meets periodically to share ideas and experiences. Another business colleague was encouraged to find a few people to serve as business mentors. Over twenty-five years ago he did that with a small group over lunch. The organization is still in existence, meets monthly and usually has over one hundred business people in attendance. The group also supports various community activities and not-for-profit organizations; many of its member serve as mentors to local college students.

When working with others, I often hear the complaint: "I don't know where groups of people meet to exchange ideas." If your research doesn't locate your desired network, why not start your own?

Understand the network's culture and live it. Like any business or organization, there is a culture in any network. If you cannot articulate the culture in a satisfactory manner to others, then you don't understand it. One of the organizations I frequent believes in and supports the concept of servant leadership. If you frequent this organization enough, you will get a sense of that and will either decide to continue to network in it or not, depending on how you feel about that concept. All organizations have a culture. Even the informal ones. Just like we discussed in the previous chapter, don't force yourself to try to fit in one that does not suit you.

Debrief yourself after you are done. Take a few minutes to summarize what you learned as a result of the networking session. Is this a group that you would like to frequent in the future? Do you have any follow-up meetings or phone calls to schedule? How was the overall experience—do you feel like you are a fit for the group? What can you do better the next time you are with this group, or at the next networking event you attend?

Recognize that not all networking is scheduled. At times when we talk about networking or listen to networking presentations, we create the impression that one must approach networking as if he or she were planning the D-day invasion. I certainly hope my ideas do not give you that impression, because I do not intend to do that. In fact, some of the best or nicest networking functions I have attended, have come up almost randomly. I have attended group functions that I never would have thought could be interesting only because I read or heard about a topic they were covering that piqued my interest. I have made some interesting and rewarding connections as a result of doing so. While there are a few groups that I like to attend regularly, I like to keep my eyes and ears open for meetings on topics that intrigue me.

It's not just about transition. For many people, the subject of networking comes up mostly in the context of job or career transition. Most of the writings about networking seem to relate to that process. But think about it. As I defined networking earlier in the chapter, networking is purposefully connecting with people. So any group getting together for sharing thoughts, learning from each other, or promoting a common purpose is also a network. People who raise money for not-for-profit organizations seek out networks of other fund raisers, of granting organizations, of potential donors. Model train builders look to meet other model train builders, train aficionados and railroad people. Movie clubs, book clubs, bowling leagues, golf groups, cooking groups—the lists go on and on—are all some sort of network. And the ideas set forth in this chapter can help you network effectively in any of them.

Humans are interdependent beings. We need each other. As I referenced in the previous chapter, John Donne said: "No man is an island . . . " Networking allows us to connect with others, to benefit from our relationships with others. And, when done correctly, networking builds valuable relationships and opportunities for both our career and our life. Good luck and good networking!

CHAPTER 14

CHANGE

Change. Such a simple word that can cause so many different reactions in people. Let me ask you. How do you feel about change? Do you welcome it, embrace it, and at times even crave it? Do you tolerate it, accept it, or deal with it? Or are you in what often seems to be the majority—you dislike it, fear it, and avoid it?

I don't know about you, but I have attended enough conferences, meetings, workshops, seminars, and webinars that try to help me appreciate, relish, or even like change. Yet, I readily acknowledge that I don't much appreciate, relish, or like it. I don't welcome it with open arms. But before you conclude that I am just a grumpy old man, I know that whether I like it or not, I have to deal with change. I cannot stop it from happening, so I need to adapt. The question remains though, just how do I do that?

I believe there are four types of people who deal with change. Those who make change happen, those who deal with change when it happens, those who watch change happen, and those who wonder what happened after a change occurs. In which category are you? Do you tend to embrace change or run wildly in the other direction?

Personally, I am more in the "deal with it" category, though I will try to "make change" in some instances. Admittedly, I have also had my share of times that I have "watched it" or "wondered what happened."

Regardless of the degree to which you like or dislike change, your willingness to accept it, or your ability to manage it, we all have to deal with change. Change will happen and you are the one who has to manage your own approach to change. No one else can "make" you change and you cannot "make" anyone else change. So, knowing that it is inevitable, what can you do? Here are some thoughts I'd like to share about dealing with change.

I believe you have to start at the beginning. And the beginning means understanding who you are and how you behave. If you know who you are and how you behave, you can better understand how you manage or respond to change. Understanding yourself and your behavior style is an important part of self-awareness. Most of us have a pretty good generic understanding of our style. But you bring it into focus when you take a more structured approach to understanding yourself. The higher your level of self-awareness, the better suited you will be to deal with change when it happens and to manage it appropriately.

An easy way to help gain a better understanding of who you are is to use a behavior assessment tool. While each of us can summarize our behavior style in our own words, a good behavior assessment tool helps you do it in a structured form. There are a wide variety of such tools out there. Over the years, I have sampled many of them. For the purposes of our discussion, I will refer to one of my favorites and one that I am sure many of you are familiar with—the DiSC®. While it may not be as sophisticated as many of the others, I find it is easy to explain, understand, and use.

The DiSC® behavioral tool was developed many years ago based on the research and writings of William Moulton Marston (1893-1947) who held a PhD in Psychology. Building on Marston's research and writings, the current version of the DiSC® assessment self-categorizes people into one of four overall behavior classes—dominant, influence, steadiness, or conscientious. Different DiSC® programs use slightly different descriptors, but they all relate back to the letters in DiSC®. My references to this behavioral tool that appear in this chapter and elsewhere in this book are taken from Everything DiSC® Facilitation System[27] by Inscape Publishing 2004 that I completed as a self-study program several years ago. Let's explore the different DiSC® behavior categories and how each of them characterizes how people deal with change.

Marston believed that people could be sorted into categories—first between those who are active or thoughtful; and second, between those who are questioning or accepting. He described each of these four categories as follows:

- Active—fast-paced, assertive, dynamic, bold

- Thoughtful—moderate-paced, calm, methodical, careful

- Questioning—logic-focused, objective, skeptical, challenging

- Accepting—people-focused, empathizing, receptive, agreeable

Once you divide a group of people into each of these two, you get four possible behavior styles:

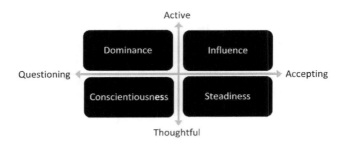

People who have a preference for the dominance behavior style are more active and questioning in their professional and personal lives. They also look at the environment as more challenging and demanding. When they are aware that change is necessary, they take action to manage it. Their individual dynamism identifies the need for a change before others; their boldness causes them to take steps to implement it. They view themselves as more powerful than or in control of their environment. They generally perceive the environment as challenging and have difficulty dealing with change that moves too slowly.

Conscientious individuals also view their environment as challenging, but because they are more thoughtful than active, they tend to behave in a more methodical and moderate-paced fashion. Their preference for dealing with change is to thoughtfully analyze it, understand it, accept it, and carefully implement it. They also prefer that change occurs in a focused and processed manner. Unlike those with dominance behaviors, conscientious people prefer that change take place at a more reasonable, sometimes slower pace. But, once they are convinced of the need for change, they will make every effort to see that change occurs in an orderly fashion.

Influencers generally view the environment as favorable. They are more people-focused; they are more concerned about the impact of change on their teams and others within the organization. They will initiate change, but want to do it in a way that has minimal effect on others. Influencers will counsel with others when managing the change processes, but they will be more than happy to leave the design of those processes to others. They work at their best when everyone is "on board" with the idea of change. They are willing to lead or manage change efforts, but would prefer that it be more of a team-oriented leadership rather than taking on sole responsibility.

People in the steadiness category also have a favorable view of the environment. Because they are more accepting than questioning, their preference is to understand the change that is necessary. Once they understand it, they are willing to work through it with the minimal amount of disruption. They would like the change process to have minimal impact on the current work flow and structure of the organization. If the organization communicates the need for the change with clarity, they will accept it and adapt accordingly. Like influencers, they are very concerned about the impact the change will have on individuals in the organization. But, if the organization has a thoughtful process for dealing with personnel issues that arise from the change, they accept it.

Understanding how you deal with change is important for you as an individual. It is also beneficial, if not critical, to understand how the people you lead deal with and manage change. If you understand the nature of the people you are leading and have an idea of how different people respond to change, then I believe you can be more effective at leading them through change.

I have used the DiSC® assessment process often to help me understand the behavior of both myself and others. However, it is not the only tool available to you. There are a variety of others that you, as the leader of a group, can add to your own leadership library. I encourage you to consider using one of these tools in your leadership role. Seek a qualified facilitator to do so.

Understanding who you are and the styles of the people you lead is the first step in dealing with change. However, whether you have detailed behavior assessments of everyone on your team or organization is not the point. The point is that people respond to the need for change differently. When you have to initiate some change in your team or organization, you should first recognize that different people with different behavior styles respond to change differently. If it is a small team, you can deal with these differences on a one-to-one basis and recognize the difference in behavior styles in doing so. If it is a large organization, you must shape your communication in a way that recognizes the different behavior styles of the group. You have to fashion your communication to give each behavior style its own WIIFM factor (what's in it for me).

Let me give you an example. A number of years ago, I had the opportunity to coach a young executive who was promoted into a significant C-suite position. Considering my exposure to him and knowledge of his behavior style, I characterized him as conscientious. He was very thoughtful in his approach to business problems and always wanted to make sure things were correct before he took action.

After he worked in his new position for a number of months, I was engaged to coach him. One of the primary areas identified for him was to be more assertive in presenting his position on issues. This was an especially important expectation of him when dealing with his fellow C-suite executives. The interviews I conducted about his behavior style clearly showed that he was a capable and talented executive in his functional area. However, one of the most frequent complaints was that he did not "speak up" often enough with his own ideas. He was not asserting himself as an equal with his peers. We worked on this development step in a very methodical manner—responding to his behavior style. We identified another C-suite executive that he held in high regard. He began to practice openly sharing his points of view on key corporate issues with this executive. He developed increasing confidence as a result of doing so and, eventually, became a more productive member of the team. They recognized that when he did speak up on key issues, it was important for them to listen to him. Normally, he had great points and suggestions to make. He successfully adapted his behavior by understanding his behavior style and applying it to his need to change. He analyzed the way he was dealing (or not dealing) with certain issues, understood the expectations of his peer group as to how he should deal with them differently, and developed his own techniques to help him change his behavior. He became more open and assertive in sharing his point of view in communications with his peer executives.

I did not make him change. Instead, by understanding his behavior style and how it related to change, I helped him create an environment in which he felt comfortable to change. Consequently, he was able to function better in his new position.

A key component to recognize when discussing change is to understand that people will not change just because you tell them to do so. People do things for their own reasons. You cannot force someone to change. You can only create an environment that communicates the need for change in a manner that they can understand and recognize their own need to do so. Once they understand the need for change, often influenced by the aforementioned WIIFM factor, they will adapt to change consistent with their respective behaviors.

I did not write this chapter to provide you with a "change management process." There are a variety of them available that you can adapt to your own style and organization. In fact, your company may have some established processes already in place to handle significant change management situations.

Instead, I wrote this chapter to offer you my thoughts about how to deal with change in yourself and lead change in others. When you are faced with a significant change that affects you, understand your own behavioral style and recognize how that can help you deal with the change. When you are leading others, recognize that each individual has their own way of responding to change. It is your responsibility as their leader to help them understand the need for change as well as to give them the support they need to come through the change process successfully. Perhaps your organization has a formal "change management" process to follow. If not, research your own and select one that helps you structure your own approach to managing change. Once you decide how you are going to manage the change, then communicate, communicate, and communicate it to your team or teams. Be aware of their need to absorb the requirements for change and the change process according to their own behavioral style. Provide opportunities for people to question what is happening. Demonstrate that you are changing right along with them. Remember to think straight and talk straight through the entire change process. This is one area of leadership in which you cannot over-communicate.

I would like to promise that if you consider and implement some of these suggestions, all of your changes going forward will be successful.

Unfortunately, I cannot promise you that, because they will not all be successful. But, I promise that you will find it is easier to change and lead others through change if you recognize differences in behavior style between yourself and those you lead.

Change happens! Change is the one certainty which you will face throughout your business life—and personal life, for that matter. The better you understand yourself and the people you lead, the better you will be able to manage the changes that will undoubtedly be a part of your career and your life.

CHAPTER 15

TRANSITION

As discussed in the previous chapter, change is inevitable. It can be big or small. Often or infrequent. It can have a large or small effect on us and our lives. One of the more frequent changes we face is transition.

Our lives are filled with transitions—births, deaths, relocations, promotions, transfers, demotions, restructurings, successful ventures, failed activities. While the ideas I talk about in this chapter apply primarily to a job or career transition, many of the thoughts can be applied to other transitional events in our lives. If you are not reading this book in succession, I encourage you to read the chapter on change if you find yourself in transition as the ideas within that chapter can help you navigate through the change you are experiencing.

Transitional change is often uncomfortable and emotional. Transitions happen whether we are ready for them or not. They happen in both our personal and professional lives. Some transitions are short lived and others are lengthy.

The transition process can sometimes seem overwhelming, but when properly approached, it is less complex than it initially seems. In this chapter, I will share my thoughts on things to consider as you manage a transition. These ideas apply to anyone in transition; someone who lost their job through uncontrollable actions, those transitioning to a new company or organization, and anyone currently transitioning or seeking to transition to a new job within their present organization.

Job transition or career transition is a major change. It is often a surprise, has complex implications, and can be very emotional. Regardless of the type of transition we go through, there is one key point to keep in mind; things will be different as a result.

In my own networking, I meet many individuals who are in job or career transition. In today's business environment the transition process is one which is ongoing and should always be in our consciousness. Even those who are fully employed should think about transition periodically. Just as we discussed in the Networking chapter, you don't want to avoid the process completely until you really need it. However, whatever your reason for transition, the first step in the process is coping with the transition.

Coping. Job loss is a major life event. Don't underestimate the effect it may have on your life. It brings with it many challenges. One of the transition groups I worked with in the past often reminded its members that people suffering job loss experienced the same stages of grief Elisabeth Kübler-Ross writes about related to the death of a loved one. Her five-stage model[28] is: denial, anger, bargaining, depression, and acceptance. In transition, the stages are often described as:

- **Shock.** Two months ago they told me I had delivered on expectations! What did I do wrong?

- **Depression and/or physical distress.** I must have performed much worse than I thought. I feel sick about this. I just want to go home and stay in bed.

- **Anger.** I knew my boss was out to get me; he has always hated my work and denigrated me in front of others. And some of my coworkers are the worst back-stabbers in the world.

- **Panic or fear.** What am I going to do? I am fifty-six years old and I am just rebuilding our retirement funds after the recession.

- **Acceptance.** Oh well, I was looking for a job when I found this one. It's time to focus my efforts on my next steps.

- **Rebuilding.** This as an opportunity to move forward. I have thought about some new skills I should acquire and I can use some of the time in my search process to work on them.

These stages are not necessarily linear. You can be in a later stage and revert to an earlier stage; but during your transition process, you will inevitably progress through all of them. It is important to keep your focus and remember that throughout the transition process, you have choices. You can let your circumstances control you, or you can control your circumstances. You are in control of your attitude and emotions. No job defines you. You define you.

Recognize the importance of the word "transition" as you work your way through it. The process will end with the old and begin with something new. There will be some hard work in between, but this in between state also provides an opportunity for you to learn and grow.

So now that you are in the transition process, how do you move forward? The transition process I describe is straightforward:

- **Assess.** Know where you are and who you are.

- **Plan.** Know where you want to go.

- **Execute.** Take the necessary actions to get where you want to go.

- **Success.** Celebrate!

Assess. In your self-assessment, first understand your economics. It is imperative that you know your financial resources and needs. If you already have a personal or family budget, review and tighten it as much as you can. If you don't have one, create one. Take a serious and honest look at your level of resources, expenditures, and potential revenues. Work with your family members to eliminate, significantly reduce, or temporarily defer all nonessential expenditures. Once you know your anticipated expenditures and projected deficit, you can project the time you have to find your next opportunity. Plan this period with plenty of cushion and identify financial support opportunities, if any. Will you need to do contract or part-time work? Might you need to borrow money from friends or family? These are difficult choices, but you should at least consider them if your circumstances call for it.

The transition process is typically stressful, and money situations will only heighten the stress level. Assessing your situation first will help you mentally prepare for the budget changes and allow you to plan accordingly.

Next, know who you are. Devote some time in the assessment process to deal with the "Who am I?" question. Invest the time to define who you are, who you want to be, and how you will get there. Through your self-assessment process, you may decide that this is the right time for you to take some risks and change careers or entertain that entrepreneurial dream. Or, it may help you solidify your plan to stay in the career you have chosen. In either case, you should allot some time to answer your own questions about who you are and where you are going.

In the chapter on change, I talk about understanding who you are behaviorally by using a behavioral analysis tool. Consider your own behavior style as you consider some of the following questions during your transition process. You may find it advantageous to write down your answers so you can refer to them throughout the transition process.

- What are your top ten values? Are they "must haves"? Does the culture of the business you are looking at seem to include these values?

- What are the five most important skills you bring to the table? How did they help you succeed in the past? What skills are you lacking to do the job or enter the career you so desire?

- What are your strengths and weaknesses?

- What do you like doing? What do you dislike doing? What do you have fun doing?

- What motivates you? What demotivates you?

- What is your preferred behavior style?

- How has your personal behavior style helped or hindered you in your past jobs?

- How do others view your behavior? How do you know? Have you asked your relatives, friends, mentors, counselors, former coworkers, clergy, coaches, or anyone else who knows you? How does what they say compare to how you see yourself?

- What careers and jobs have you had?

- What has worked? What has not worked?

- What hobbies and interests do you have?

Once you have answered these self-analysis questions, look more specifically at your career direction. Do you have a career direction? If not, these questions can help you create one:

- What career do you desire? Is it industry-specific, functional-specific, geographic-specific?

- Where are you in relation to your career? Are you making your career or is your career making you?

- What career paths interest you? How can you transfer your skills and experience?

- Should you take a career assessment to help you find a direction?

- How does your self-assessment align with the career you chose?

- How do your past performance evaluations align with the career you chose?

- What careers and jobs have you had?

- What has worked? What has not worked?

- What careers and jobs would you like to have?

- What hobbies and interests do you have?

Decide which of these are most important to you. Develop your own format or technique for documenting answers and analyzing what they tell you about yourself. Some use a journal, some use an Excel spreadsheet, some use sticky notes, others design their own special technique. Whatever method you choose, use something to gather your thoughts throughout the process. Once you have completed this self-analysis, begin to develop your plan.

Plan and execute. Once your assessment is done, consider the following steps as a part of your planning process, but recognize that they may not all apply to your situation or happen in the order presented.

Timeline. Get started by creating a timeline for yourself. Connect it to the analysis of how much time you need before your economic resources are at risk. Use that end time to set quarterly, monthly, weekly, and even daily goals. Do whatever works best for you and devise your own process for monitoring yourself against those goals. Hold yourself accountable to your process. The process will not work without accountability. Consider enlisting a friend, colleague, spouse, or other partner to check in with you periodically to monitor your progress.

There are a variety of things you should do while in the transition process. The following chart represents my point of view on the effectiveness of different activities to conduct during your transition process. Plan and allocate your time sensibly.

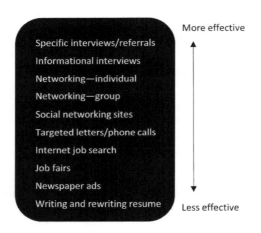

Targets. Once you have a timeline created, it is important to identify your target market. Research industries, careers, contacts, and networking groups to help you decide which best fit your self-assessment. Identify associations and special interest groups in those industries to target for specific networking. Develop a target list of companies you would like to visit for informational or formal interviews. Locate individuals you know in the industries and companies you have identified. If you cannot identify specific individuals, or do not have direct access to them, identify others that you feel might help you reach your targets.

Prepare lists that you can share with others as you network. When you share your target list with someone, don't just ask them if they have any contacts to the organization; ask them if they know of any other similar organizations you should consider. Many people incorporate their target list in a one-page document called a handbill. Similar to a one-page resume, the top third includes a summary of your key experiences and abilities; the middle third includes your specific most recent work experiences; the final third includes your target list of specific industries and companies. Identify functional areas of interest—those in which you have expertise and those in which you would like to gain expertise.

Self-accountability. Earlier I mentioned that your plan should be broken down in time blocks—quarterly, monthly, weekly, daily. Do this in a manner that suits your own style. Hold yourself accountable to this timetable. It also helps to have someone else help you hold yourself accountable. Use your circle of relatives, friends, and colleagues to assist you.

One note on accountability measures: if you set a goal to make ten direct phone calls and have three networking visits in the next week and you fall short of that target, don't assume that you have to double your efforts the following week. Many people "beat themselves up" if they don't achieve their periodic goals in the transition process. Don't waste your time regretting what you didn't do. Accept it and move on. And, when you have some success like scoring an interview or an informational visit with a company, feel free to celebrate it!

Resumes. Part of the transition process requires you to have an appropriate resume. It has been my experience, though, that when I speak to groups about transition, they often want to focus solely on the resume. This is, in fact, important. However, there are other steps in the transition process that are equally, if not more, important. So, I wrote a separate chapter on resumes that you will find later in this book.

Networking. Managing through a transition is mostly about networking, networking, networking. It is the most important activity you can do, which is why I have addressed the topic of networking in its own chapter. I agree that while some transitions are successful by posting your resume to websites, the Internet should serve as one tool in the process, but not the only tool. All major surveys I have seen indicate that your primary efforts in any transition process should be devoted to networking. You should do it as much as possible—to help others and to help yourself. Devote the largest portion of your search time identifying representatives of your target organizations and setting up times to meet them. Your local community has any number of effective, high-energy groups with which you can associate to expand your business network. Identify them and participate in them. In addition to the traditional transition groups, don't forget business trade associations, college alumni organizations, local faith-based groups, social clubs, friends, neighbors, and relatives. You never know who knows whom. Naturally, your networking should be focused and aligned with your overall targets. Occasionally, networking with those who are not on your primary radar screen can be quite rewarding. You never know where the next opportunity exists. Remember, " . . . chance favors the prepared mind."[29]

Use group networking to meet individuals with whom you can network on a direct and professional level. These meetings can either be for specific opportunities or for informational interviews. The more opportunities you have to present yourself to individuals, the more likely you will be successful. However, networking is not all about groups. If the transition you are planning is internal to the organization, networking with others—your boss, your colleagues, your mentor, your coach—can be the most important step in your process.

I am often asked if you should network with search executives and professionals. Yes, you should try to do so. But remember, their primary task is to serve their client (the company who is the potential employer) and find the right person to fill a need. They cannot spend much of their time networking with you, unless you have the potential to fill that need, so while they can be an avenue to try, you should not rely on them exclusively.

Again, remember what we have already covered—networking is not just about you. The primary focus of networking is to help others. Keep that in mind for every networking meeting or conversation you have.

While networking is the most important activity in your job or career search, don't forget other channels available to market yourself, identify potential opportunities, and create leads—cold calls and letters, job boards and websites, newspaper ads, etc. While these should not consume most of your time, you should devote some measure of activity to them. Opportunities can, and do, come from anywhere. So, I recommend that a small portion of your transition time be allocated to website searches, Internet postings, etc.

It is important to remember that networking does not only apply when you are in transition to a new company. It also applies within a business. Build the habit of networking within your company. It helps build relations, makes you visible to others within your organization and increases your knowledge of how business operates.

Interview. Once you have secured a face-to-face interview, here are several ideas to consider:

- Prepare, prepare, prepare. Plan it, practice it, re-plan it, and practice it again. Develop your own questions and rehearse them with a colleague, friend, family member, coach, or mentor.

- Know the company and how you intend to fit in. Research it and, if possible, research your interviewer. Research aids you can use include: Internet searches, business and social websites, other social media, annual reports, SEC filings, business newspapers, and other people who may know something about the company, organization or person. (e.g., relatives, friends, neighbors, colleagues, church members, clubs, fraternities, colleges, etc.)

- Organize your thoughts. Have a plan with your own points you wish to get across in the interview. Direct the conversation and your responses back to those message points.

- Tell the truth, don't apologize, and don't feel the need to provide "context" unless absolutely necessary to make a point. And even then, better to ask the interviewer if they need context.

- Be on time. Timeliness starts with you. Whether you are attending a meeting or running a meeting, you should be prompt and ready to go at the scheduled time, even if others are not.

If you are doing a telephone interview, all of the above steps apply with consideration of a few more:

- Make sure the technology works. Cell phones and speaker phones are great, but you have to be certain the reception is clear and consistent. If you have any doubts about the quality of the reception, use a land line.

- Do the interview from a quiet place with no distractions. It is easiest to do this, I am sure, at a quiet place in your home. But if there is a risk of background noise or interruptions, select somewhere else that provides you the peacefulness you will need to focus.

- Have your tools available (e.g., pen, paper, etc.). Have the questions you prepared at hand for easy reference.

- Visualize the person on the other end.

- Observe your own expressions in a mirror.

- Don't be afraid to stand up; walk around and gesture—let the energy work for you. You don't need to be frozen in your chair.

- Minimize one-word answers and negative verbs.

- Never, never, never multitask during the interview.

Behaviorals. Whether the interview is in-person or on the telephone, you will often receive some behavioral questions. For example: The interviewer asks how you handled a particular situation or accomplished a particular task in the past. Don't respond with a hypothetical. If they ask you, "How did you accomplish X?" don't respond, "This is how I would do X." Respond, "This is how I accomplished X." If you have never accomplished X before, acknowledge it and describe a similar situation in which you accomplished Y.

Here are a few types of behavioral scenarios you might hear:

- Describe what you did when you worked on a team in which one member did not fulfill their responsibilities.

- Tell me how you handled a situation in which a boss, peer, direct report or a customer made an insensitive or off-color remark.

- Describe a work crisis you have faced in the past and how you handled it (deadline accelerated; requirement to work when you had personal plans; etc.).

- What have you done when you have been instructed to perform a task or resolve an issue in a way that is inconsistent with your personal values?

Remember, the interviewer wants to know what you actually did. Do not respond with a hypothetical, "This is how I would handle it," answer. Be prepared for behavioral questions and always practice answering behavioral questions during your rehearsal process.

Listening. Practice your best listening skills. I have included other thoughts on listening in a separate chapter, but I will repeat a few of them here as a reminder:

- Show that you are interested in and care about the person to whom you are speaking.

- Use effective body language, gestures, facial expressions, or voice tones.

- Encourage the other person to talk as much as possible. Remember that silence is your friend.

- Make sure you understand what the other person says, use the techniques of repeating or reframing for clarification. Understand the context and ask questions to clarify. Listen for what is not being said; pay attention to body language, facial expressions, or voice tones of the other person in the conversation.

Other tools. I have mentioned different tools you can use in your transition process throughout this chapter. For networking, I encourage the use of networking sites like LinkedIn to make connections and learn about people you might have the chance to meet. In addition, there are many books that can help you in the transition process, but there are three that specifically come to mind, and which I use frequently when discussing a transition process:

- John Lucht's *Rites of Passage at $100,000 to $1 Million+: Your Insider's Lifetime Guide to Executive Job-Changing and Faster Career Progress in the 21st Century*. I have read different portions of it and find it to be a tremendous reference source for anyone going through the transition process.

- Keith Ferazzi's *Never Eat Alone*. This is a great book on networking that everyone should use, and not just during the job transition process.

- Michael Watkins' *The First 90 Days*. Once you land your next big opportunity, whether in a new company or within your current company, I recommend you peruse a copy of this book.

While each of these books may seem like they are written with a heavy focus on the C-suite or senior executive level, they are full of great, easily adaptable ideas for helping you adapt to and assimilate into your new role quickly.

Appearances. Appearances do count, yet there is no doubt that over my 40+ years in business, dress codes have changed. You don't very often walk into a corporate organization environment anymore and see men in suits, button-down shirts, and ties or women in similar business-related dress. But when you are going on an interview, meeting someone for networking purposes, or visiting a company for an informational interview, consider the following:

- Evaluate the setting; consider the nature of the business; ask about a dress code. If they tell you it is business casual or casual, ask what that means.

- When in doubt, dress conservatively.

- Consider the position you wish to fill and dress one-to-two levels higher. Once you get the job, you will be in a better position to evaluate appropriate daily business dress.

- Make sure your clothes are appropriately cleaned and pressed and that they comfortably fit and that your shoes are clean (and polished if they are the type of shoes that take polish).

- Check the grooming of your hair and nails.

- Just say no to sandals, flip-flops, tight clothes, golf shirts. Even if you visit the business ahead of time and see this type of dress, don't assume that they expect this is appropriate for an interview.

- Make judicious use of perfume, cologne, hair spray, makeup, and jewelry.

- Check the Internet—Google has over one million hits on "How to dress for a job interview."

Social media. I am the last person to advise you on how to use social media. I have been accused as being rather a Neanderthal in the use of such tools. But they are valuable, and they are becoming more and more recognized and used by those managing the transition process. Use them appropriately and carefully. And remember that once your thoughts and words are out there on the "cloud," it is likely they will be there for a long time.

Remember yourself. Throughout your transition process take care of yourself. Get regular exercise. Manage your diet. Though looking for a position is a 40-hour-a-week job, don't be afraid to take some time off. When you have a success in a great networking meeting or interview, reward yourself.

Share your experiences with others. Speak about your situation regularly with your spouse or partner. If you have children, I encourage you to make sure to periodically include them in the conversation about what is going on in the transition process. Keep it relevant to their age level, but help them understand what is happening so they are not victimized by playground or social media rumors about "mom not working" or "dad being out of a job."

If you have a favorite hobby, don't think you have to give it up during your transition process—just be careful that it does not take over too much of your time. Use other techniques like yoga or meditation to bring some tranquility into your life. If you are a person of faith, take advantage of your faith to help you through this process. If you find yourself slipping into severe negativity or potential depression, talk to a professional who helps others deal with those circumstances.

Coaching. Finally, many ask if they should engage a coach in their transition process. Before that step, I believe there are many good organizations that can provide support in the process—networking groups, professional and trade associations, faith-based organizations, college alumni organizations, to name a few. I am sure there are numerous such organizations in your local community. However, if you are stuck, or need help beyond the support organizations that are readily available, there are qualified coaches in the marketplace who can serve you. Many communities have local chapters of the International Coach Federation, or other similar coaching organizations. Very often their websites have "Find-A-Coach" help.

Success. At the end of this process, you will find "Success!!!" When you achieve it, celebrate it! Do whatever works for you to help you absorb the fact that you are starting a new chapter in both your career and your life. Allow yourself time to recover and recharge. And be sure to share the success with those you love.

It is becoming more and more of a truism that people in business today will have multiple careers and multiple job experiences. I believe this is accurate and that you should prepare yourself and shape this process for yourself—as you will likely have to do it again, multiple times. And remember, it is your process! Own it. It is not always easy and I won't try to convince you that it is an adventure. But take on the challenge. Don't allow yourself to be stuck in the past. Instead look to the future and the opportunities that lie ahead. You may just look back on this transition process someday and see the positivity that resulted.

CHAPTER 16

RESUMES

As we spend some time talking about networking, transitioning, and entrepreneurship, one of the tools you will utilize is your resume. If someone asked you today to show them your resume, would you be able to pull up a current file and send it to them? If you are like most people, the answer is, "No." Most resumes are out of date, unable to be located, or simply unavailable.

In today's ever-changing environment, your resume should be ready at any time. Some believe it should even be in the market at all times. That, however, is your personal choice. At the very least, you should have it ready and available within your electronic reach in a moment's notice.

As you have learned elsewhere in this book, I spent a significant number of years in the first chapter of my life at a professional firm known as Arthur Andersen, or Andersen in its later years. And, many of you also know that this firm came to a rather dark ending in 2002. Although the firm no longer exists, we do have a fairly active group of alumni. At one of our get-togethers, a former colleague of mine raised the following question: "Is being a former Arthur Andersen employee an asset or liability when I look for a new job? I know it has been awhile since the firm has disappeared, but I would like to know if my association with the firm is negatively affecting my job opportunities."

In an informal survey I conducted, several alums from around the globe responded to this question and they were almost all resoundingly positive. I have also asked the same question of several search executives and professional recruiters. As I read through the responses, I thought to ask the question: "How does anyone handle an inconvenient truth like this on their resume?" A question like this often comes up when working with people who are transitioning jobs and careers.

First, let me clarify what I mean by an inconvenient truth. I am not talking about the 2006 movie documentary of the same name. I use the term "inconvenient truth" because I think it is an accurate term that describes facts we may not like to talk about during the transition process. From Dictionary.com, "inconvenient" is synonymous with "annoying, awkward, bothersome"[30] and "truth" is simply "a verified or indisputable fact."[31] Inconvenient truths exist in our past; often, we just hope they will go away or be ignored. They are experiences that we think may be negative to search executives, recruiters, or potential employers. They are true because they happened. They are inconvenient because we prefer not to mention them on our resume or discuss them in an interview.

For example, a young man or woman might be out of the work force for an extended period to care for an elderly or ill parent or even to battle a serious illness or disease of their own. Or either parent might voluntarily remove themselves from the workforce for a number of years to care for children. None of these circumstances should have an effect on a hiring decision. However, others have often commented to me that they are concerned about how, or if, this should be presented in a resume.

As you know, I believe in thinking straight and talking straight. I believe such advice applies here. If you have a gap in your resume between jobs or careers, the facts that support that gap should be explained. Truth should fill the gap. Unfilled gaps in a resume only cause lost time and productivity on the part of anyone who reviews your resume. They waste time trying to figure out what was in the gap. The interviewer might think you are hiding something. Worse yet, they may presume the missing link is negative, and toss your resume aside. Examples of descriptions that relate to these situations may be as follows:

- "1996-1998. Cared for two elderly relatives who were suffering from long-term and debilitating diseases. Attended the following seminars and workshops to maintain business knowledge..."

- "2001-2002. Out of the workforce for twelve months to assist spouse with baby twins born in January 2001."

- "2003-2005. Under doctor's orders, unable to work due to health-related issues, which have since been completely corrected. Enrolled in the following self-study programs to maintain and upgrade relevant technical knowledge in …"

- "2000-2010. Stay at home mom. Managed the household and self-developed the following skills: scheduling, budgeting, and organizing, logistics management, personnel counseling. Enhanced time management skills and the ability to work well with others through volunteer activities."

It is important to explain similar gaps in your resume. My preference is to do it on the resume itself. Others might say do it in your cover letters or other resume transmittals. If you include it, and a recruiter wants to ask about it, she can. At least the recruiter won't be trying to guess what is missing!

For example, returning to the question my colleague asked whether working for Arthur Andersen was an asset or a liability. Don't try to deal with the tarnished reputation of a prior organization or event on your resume. I recently spoke to an executive who had worked a number of years with a business. The owner of that business had a very negative reputation. This executive felt that the negative reputation of the owner was affecting his ability to present himself in certain interview situations. I agree that is a difficult situation. My best advice is not to change or alter the facts of your employment on the resume. Instead, confidently deal with the recruiters concerns in your interview.

Remember, your resume should always be factually correct. If you believe your experience at any company carries a negative connotation for your professional reputation, plan to address it during the interview. Organize your thoughts and rehearse your comments. Naturally, you cannot know what is in your recruiter's head. You can only ask if they require some clarification about your experience with the company. Plan your response accordingly. The more prepared you are to answer these types of questions, the more confident you will be in your delivery and explaining these inconvenient truths.

Regardless of what your inconvenient truths are, it is essential to remember that employers want to know where you are now, where you are headed and what you can do for them. It is true that our past has a huge impact on our present and our future. Use the experiences you have had to build your advantage. Use the interview—not the resume— as an opportunity to explain to the interviewer how past experiences will enable you to excel in the position being offered. Remember, the interviewer wants an accurate, fact-based resume that describes any gaps that exist and accounts for your overall career path. Your cover letters and the interviews themselves will provide the necessary context to the facts in the resume.

For example, a client of mine was being interviewed for a job and she had a two-year gap in her work experience. She had a comment on her resume that briefly described the two-year gap as a period in which she was caring for an elderly parent. She told me the subject came up in some of her interviews. When it did, she explained that she often had to deal with a government agency and insurance company on behalf of the parent. The experience she gained enhanced her research and organizational skills. She also felt it helped her build her skills in presenting factual arguments and carrying them to successful resolution. By being prepared with a straightforward, fact-based statement about her experiences during that time frame, she successfully moved the conversation from the "gap" to a discussion of what she learned from the experience and how it benefited her business skills for the future.

We all have inconvenient truths in our past. Plan your response to them for your interview. When they come up in your transition or search, deal with them accurately and precisely. Don't dwell on them. Use what you learned from dealing with them to help build your skills for the future.

I believe the issue of inconvenient truths is one of the most important ones you deal with when preparing your resume. Maybe you don't have any. But if you do, I hope my ideas help. Let's take a look at other resume questions I've received.

How long should my resume be? Recruiters and search executives tell me a resume should be two pages, maximum. Personally, I disagree. If it goes slightly beyond two pages, chances are low that the recruiter will disregard the resume based on length. Don't spend enormous amounts of time trying to cram thirty years of business experience into two pages and then worry about what you may have left out. Your resume should tell your story more than a CNN news item, but less than a Dostoevsky novel. However, if you are strongly committed to a two-page max, focus mainly on the prior ten years of experience and summarize earlier years in less detail. But always include a brief summary of the earlier years at the end of the primary ten years. You should always account for the period from your college completion to present day. And, don't forget to fill the non-work gaps as indicated in the previous examples.

Additionally, don't try to fit your resume on two pages by reducing the font size to such a point that it is difficult to read. If someone researching resumes has to squint to read yours, they will most likely set it aside and move on to the next document.

Should my resume be chronologically, functionally, or industry-focused? Most recruiters prefer a chronological resume, with your most recent experiences shown first. Each section briefly describes the company and industry, your titles, responsibilities, and accomplishments. A functional resume—one that focuses on functional areas of responsibility such as finance, market, research, etc., —is generally not preferred.

What can I do to save space and keep it at 2-3 pages? Save space on your resume by eliminating superlatives. After all, who isn't a "strategically focused, visionary leader" or a "profit-generating and innovative executive" who can "skillfully lead a team of high-performers focused on meeting the company's goals?" Your resume should be grounded in facts. Your accomplishments should be clearly stated. Accomplishments should be rationally measured; for example, "Implemented a standard cost system in a manufacturing division that resulted in $23 million of annual, documented cost savings." I agree all accomplishments cannot be quantified. But, they should be as fact-based and accurate as possible. Clearly describe your accomplishments. If you can factually state the benefits of those accomplishments, it is even better.

Should I have separate resumes for different industries or types of jobs? This is where I differ with a lot of good recruiters and search personnel. I am not a big fan of multiple resumes. That probably comes from my own inability to keep myself organized and my fear that I might send the wrong resume in response to a specific search. From my perspective, you are who you are. You have accomplished what you have accomplished. Your resume should tell a factual story. Do your selling in your cover letters and your interviews, not on your resume. If you feel your resume does not represent an exact "fit" to the stated job requirements, modify your cover letter accordingly.

How do I "sell" or "market" myself in a resume? You don't. Your resume should be a fact-based response to the position description. It should be the truth about your background and experiences. Use your cover letters and interviews to promote your worth to the potential employer.

Do I have to show dates of employment, graduation, etc., on my resume? Yes. Absolutely and unequivocally show such dates. I have not met a recruiter or search executive that responds warmly to a resume without them. If you are concerned that including dates of your graduation and other employment will yield information—perhaps, like how old you are—accept the fact and move on. You can deal with your age in the interview by discussing your skills, experience and ability to adapt to new situations. Don't give the recruiter an opportunity to think that you are trying to conceal something.

Where can I get help preparing my resume? There are numerous sources of reference to help you with resume questions—books, blogs, newsletters, Internet sites. Networking groups often have examples of good resumes. In addition, there are businesses that will help you build your resume for a fee. However, let me caution you to be extra careful if you go this route. If you choose to hire someone to help with your resume, make sure you have a clear understanding of your expectations versus theirs. I also suggest that you ask those who know you the best (colleagues, friends, family) to review your resume. They can be surprisingly helpful if you give them the chance to help. They know you better than an individual in a firm and can help you think of things you might have overlooked. They can help you say things in a way that is more "you" than "resume-speak." And most of them appreciate the opportunity to help.

Once you have completed your resume, stick with it. Don't rewrite it based on every suggestion you receive from someone. Most importantly, keep your updated resume handy at all times. Make changes and additions when they happen and know where it is at all times. Remember, resumes are important, but they don't get you the job—you get you the job. Nobody ever hired a resume.

CHAPTER 17

————

DOING YOUR OWN THING

When was the last time you thought about your job? Or, your career? Do you like what you are doing? Where you are going? Do you need a change? Are you ready for a change? When you have these thoughts do you dream big? Do you consider a job change or a career change or both? Do you ever dream about "doing your own thing"?

Many surveys I have seen in recent years point to increases in the number of people who attempt to strike out on their own. Call them temporary workers, freelancers, or contract workers, it seems more and more people are looking at "business free agency" as an option in their lives.

In my executive coaching practice, I meet with many people going through the transition process and I am often asked, "What should I think about when striking out on my own?" In this chapter, I will share some of my observations about doing your own thing. My comments are focused mostly on the individual who wants to provide services, because that has been my personal experience. But, the general concepts are also applicable when bringing a new product to the marketplace.

There are many great books available describing the proper steps to take and which processes to follow to become an entrepreneur. There are also many considerations—legal, ownership, structure, process, people, etc. These specific topics often require support or advice from professionals in those fields. My thoughts within this chapter are more geared toward exploring the personal thoughts and ideas for you to consider as you plan to go out on your own. Even if you are not planning to take the risk of full entrepreneurship, I believe you will find these ideas helpful.

Understand your economics. If you are considering doing your own thing, the first question you must answer is: Do you understand your economics? Will your personal financial situation allow you time to do some exploration? If the answer is a resounding "no," then focus first on getting the best job you can to stabilize your economic side. Save the "do-your-own-thing" for later. Don't disregard it, just put it on hold temporarily. Get your economic side in balance before exploring new, riskier opportunities.

Shortly after I started my coaching practice, I was doing some volunteer coaching work in a transition organization. I had a meeting with one of the program participants to discuss his job, career needs, and aspirations. We spent an entire meeting in which I led him through the lofty goals of setting long-term aspirations and the difficulties of focusing on that long-term objective. Near the end of our scheduled time, I happened to ask him about his current economic situation. He responded, "Well, Ed, if I don't find a job by the end of next month, I will lose my apartment lease and will have to start living out of my car or a shelter."

I learned my lesson. Now, whenever I have a serious discussion with someone going through job or career transition, I first ask if they have their economic situation under control. Do they know how long they can go, if necessary, before they must start collecting a paycheck? It's a sensitive question, but I think a coach should ask it to understand the context of the person's needs. And, if you are the person being coached, you should not be afraid or ashamed to let the coach know what your economic situation is—not in great detail, but enough detail to give your coach an overall perspective so that they are able to provide you with the best advice given your personal situation.

As a part of understanding your economics, you need to develop a budget. Know how much you spend and how much you need. Note I said, "need." If you are truly serious about going out on your own, approach your life realistically. This may mean recognizing that you don't "need" to spend an exorbitant amount of money each morning on a fancy beverage that makes you "feel" good when a simpler alternative will do. You don't have to give up all the fancy stuff, but it might be a good idea to reduce or control your spending on some things as you make this transition.

Economic plans can be as elaborate or as simple as you want to make them. There are plenty of financial planning tools available in the marketplace if you want to develop a comprehensive financial budget. Or, if your style is more back-of-the-envelope, you can go that route as well. Just make sure you consider all your expenditure needs. Once you know how much you need to support your downsized lifestyle, simply compare that to what you have, including income you believe you can generate during the process of starting your own business. You will then have an idea of how long you can live comfortably while you try to achieve the success of building your own business.

Know your skills. Once you have a good understanding of your economics, create a realistic inventory of the skills you need to bring your service to the marketplace. Ask yourself some of these questions:

- Are your skills unique or special in any particular way?

- If not, how are you going to separate yourself from others in the field? Or is the market large enough that you don't need to separate yourself that much from other service providers?

- What do you bring to the table that no one else does?

- Is there a market out there for what you do? Or will you have to create a demand for your services?

- Will you need any support or assistance to perform functions that are not a part of the unique abilities you will offer to your clients?

- What is the potential life cycle of the service you will provide?

For example, if you are skilled at helping others prepare and file their income taxes, you will probably have a readily available market to ply your trade for many years to come. However, if you are a specialist in a specific area of state sales taxes and the law changes dramatically to eliminate the need for the specialty you have, you must be able to quickly change horses to provide services that your clients need in order to keep your business afloat.

As you plan your business, think about the life cycle of the service you are going to provide. If you create a business to respond to a specific new marketplace need, you may be challenged to adapt your skills to different needs if the market demand wanes.

Know your values. Another important, but often overlooked step, is to know and understand your own values. As my friend and colleague John Blumberg asked in his book, *Good to the Core - Building Value with Values,* what is your core? What are the key life principles you have? Which do you value so greatly that you will not compromise them in any aspect of your life?[32] Compiling this list of values will take time. Don't rush it. Think about it, share your list with others close to you, and refine it. But don't take forever to assemble it or you won't make it through the planning process. You can polish your list as you go. If you struggle with this, John's aforementioned book has some great suggestions to help you.

Once you know your values it is important to never, never, never compromise them. You can do your best to avoid situations that may tempt you to compromise your values, but you will not always be able to do so. Remember, you alone make the decision of whether you will compromise them; no one else forces you to do so.

Create a vision and build a plan. If you are serious about going out to the marketplace on your own, it is important that you have a vision of what it is that you aspire to be. Give some thought to this. Visualize how you want your life to look in twenty, thirty, or even fifty years and beyond. Scientists and researchers tell us that if we take care of our health, we are likely to live longer than our preceding generations.

Start with this simple, thought provoking exercise: Picture yourself celebrating your century mark birthday. Your friends and relatives are gathered with you to celebrate this occasion. They are toasting your life. Some of them know you professionally, some personally. What are they are saying about you? What do you hope they are saying about you?

Summarize these thoughts and use them to begin to create your vision. For example, do you want to be:

- The best professional golfer the world has ever known and break all existing records?

- An engineer who is recognized as a major contributor to the science of biochemical engineering?

- A librarian who is recognized in his community as a source of reference knowledge and support for young people who are attempting to expand their education?

- A bus driver who has served his community all his life and transported people to their destinations safely throughout?

- A respected professional golfer who is successful on the LPGA tour and used her talents to train young women in the skills of golf?

- A father or mother who has raised their children in a manner that reflects their beliefs and values?

Once you have your vision in mind, keep it in front of you. Remind yourself of it periodically. Some people post it on a wall, while others use their electronic calendars to read it daily. Some include it in their email addresses. Whatever your technique is, do something to regularly remind you of what your vision is.

After you have created your vision, develop a plan to move forward. I am not going to discuss the details of building a plan here. There are plenty of tools available on the Internet, at the bookstore, or at the library to assist you. I encourage you to find one that fits your style and use it. And, the more frequently you can refer to it and hold yourself accountable against it, the more success you will have.

Admittedly, I am not the world's greatest planner. In fact, I would probably have to struggle to get out of the bottom quartile. I just know that when I engage in the rigors of planning, I accomplish more. I encourage you to do the same, and I feel confident that you will also accomplish more when you have a plan.

Once you have a plan that you are comfortable with, start executing. Don't wait for the perfect plan. It doesn't exist. And, be flexible and prepared to modify your plan because things will always change in the process.

A key element of your plan should be your specific goals. Remember the SMART acronym—Specific, Measurable, Achievable, Realistic, and Timely.

For example, consider our LPGA professional golfer example who has set her vision as: "To be a respected professional golfer who is successful on the LPGA tour and used her talents to train young women in the skills of golf." Four goals that reflect greater specificity might be:

- **Personal.** To be sufficiently successful to live in a golfing community that provides the amenities of a professional and personal life that I prefer.

- **Professional.** To have won at least five tournaments on the LPGA tour and at least one major tournament by age 35 and to leverage those victories into my own training academy for young women golfers.

- **Physical.** To manage my health in a manner that allows me to fulfill the personal and professional goals I have set out. This includes appropriate diet and exercise, regular doctor visits, etc.

- **Spiritual.** To identify my core values and beliefs and practice them regularly.

The more you can set specific goals, the easier it is to be self-accountable and measure your progress. And finally, keep your specific goals simple!

Establish your timeline. Start your plan with an overall idea of where you would like to end up ten, twenty, even thirty years down the road. This is your life you are talking about. Look ahead and create your future. Then fill the gaps and build in the steps to achieve it. For example, if you set lofty goals for thirty years out, then break those goals down into ten-year increments. Take the first ten-year increment and split it into two five-year pieces. Take the first five-year piece and create five one-year sets of goals. Break down the first year into quarters, the first quarter into months, and the first month into weeks. Then develop a daily plan that builds back up into the weeks, months, quarters, and years. Devote some time periodically to review and update things. This sounds like a lot of planning time, but once you form the habit, it is relatively easy to do.

Decide what accountability periods work for you and establish your goals accordingly. Some people have daily goals, while others have weekly or monthly goals. The process I have suggested starts at the end and works back to today. Do what suits your personality, your style and then hold yourself accountable. Share your goals with a partner or a friend, if you wish, but don't pass off the accountability to someone else.

The process may sound overwhelming at first. But once you get into it, you will find that it is not. And once you have identified a process for yourself, even if you let it slip for a while, you will be able to get back into it with relative ease.

Consider all aspects of your life. While most of the thoughts in this chapter relate to going out on your own to start your business, don't forget the other aspects of your life as a part of your planning process. What part of your life and your plan relates to your family, your friends, and your community? Are you viewing your future as one segmented by a period of work and then a period of retirement? Do you think you will be blending the two throughout your life? As you plan to do your own thing, recognize the personal, physical, emotional, and spiritual needs and challenges you may face along the way.

Maintain your focus. I learned a very valuable lesson years ago when I struck out on my own. As I began to develop my own business, I considered offering executive coaching and speaking services. Consequently, I found myself responding to all sorts of requests for different engagements. Some of this was driven out of my desire to simply generate work. But in reflecting on my behavior, I realize that much of it had to do with my own style. I enjoy trying different things in my practice. In fact, I enjoy trying new things in life. Instead of always going to my favorite restaurant and ordering a regularly enjoyed meal, I prefer to try a new restaurant and order something I have never had before. I like new things. I am distracted by what's new and exciting and this can cause me to lose focus.

As I continued to develop my service business, I learned that I needed to narrow my focus. As a result, I decided not to focus on becoming a professional speaker and instead to focus on working with others as an executive coach or mentor because it is more personally rewarding.

So, remember to maintain your focus. Set a specific goal and stay on that path. Go for it. If you need periodic reminders to stay on your path, then ask someone—friend, spouse, close relative, business associate, or mentor to remind you.

Don't sell work, build relationships. This subtitle should be self-explanatory, but I am amazed at how often we violate it. I have attended many professional selling or product sales workshops in my lifetime. Every one of them talks about the importance of building relationships with potential customers or clients. Yet, in my coaching practice, I cannot tell you how many times I am presented with comments such as "So-and-so doesn't care about the customer," or "She doesn't want to have long-term relationships; she just wants to get the sale and move on," or "He's only interested in his own production; he won't lift a hand to help others." Another point I find interesting—no one who sees this problem sees it in themselves, but they can always see it in someone else.

A colleague of mine who runs his own leadership development company tells the following story. He received a call from a large, multi-location company inquiring if he would be interested in bidding on a significant leadership development project for the executives and other leaders in the company. His was, essentially, a five-person company. He agreed to submit a proposal. After his written proposal made the cut, he was invited to give an oral presentation. The day of the meeting, he sat outside the company's conference room waiting for his turn. The room had interior and exterior windows, so my friend could follow the action like a silent movie. In the meeting room were about eight of the company's senior executives in the midst of receiving an oral presentation from one of the largest consulting firms in the world. There were seven representatives from the consulting company present. He nervously waited outside and observed as all seven of the consultants delivered their share of the massive Power Point presentation. He kept looking at his three-page note summary and wondered if he even had a chance. By now, you may have guessed the outcome. My friend's company won the proposal.

He was flabbergasted yet incredibly pleased with his victory. In a later debriefing, the client explained that his proposal focused on listening to their needs, asking probing questions about their needs, and restating and reframing the issues in a way that the client's executives felt they were being understood. He spent little time talking about his company's successes and the generic "benefits" he could provide. His emphasis on building a relationship resonated with them and made him the best fit for their company.

Relationships are essential to the success of your business. Failing to build relationships can be extremely costly to your business so listen to your customer and meet their needs. While building relationships is time consuming it is always well worth the investment.

Quality should be job 1. As I mentioned in an earlier chapter, Ford Motor Co. had an advertising campaign built around the slogan "Quality is Job 1." I do not know how effective this campaign was for Ford specifically, but I believe in this message for every business. Whether you build a product or deliver a service, customers will reward your business with success if you meet their expectations. I have not met a customer who does not want the product you sell them or the service you provide them to satisfy their expectations. It is really that simple.

So ask yourself, how do you define quality? Do your customers want quality in the product or service they buy from you? How do you know? Have you asked them? Have you asked them what they mean by "quality"? No doubt there are extremely successful businesses that "create a market" by giving the consumer a product or service that they did not know they needed. But most businesses succeed because they provide a product or service that meets or exceeds customer expectations. They determine expectations and seek to meet them.

The business landscape is littered with failed entities that lost their way regarding the quality of their product or service. Quality failure can damage your brand irrevocably. Commit to quality in your product and service delivery and never compromise. Don't shortchange it to save money or appease a certain customer or a group of customers. The long-term effects of doing so can be devastating.

Know yourself and your people. I believe that most successful entrepreneurs and business people know themselves; they know their strengths and weaknesses very well. But I am not always sure that they know their behavior style well enough to know how their behavior and leadership habits affect others. I have mentioned this in other chapters and believe it bears repeating here.

As part of doing your own thing, I recommend you invest a little time and money to better understand your behavior style. Even though this may only reaffirm your self-knowledge, it is a good reminder of what your behavior style is and how others tend to see you. As you grow your business, have those you hire take the same behavior assessment that you do. Then, share the results with each other and talk about how you can use this knowledge to work better in groups and teams.

There are hundreds of behavior assessments in the marketplace. Pick one that you will use in your business. Make it a part of your hiring and employee development process. Administer it consistently across the business and encourage employees to share their results with others.

Use the results of your assessment to understand your own strengths and weaknesses. When you start out, you will have to do almost everything yourself. However, try to minimize the amount of time you spend on items that don't relate to your strengths. Identify the skills you need to operate your business that are not in your "wheelhouse." As you grow your business, hire someone else to do these tasks.

The activities you pursue as you build your business can generally be broken down into three categories:

- Activities that are essential to grow your business and that you perform extremely well.

- Activities that are essential to grow your business and that you need help to accomplish because they are not among your principal talents.

- All other activities that are necessary to run your business.

As you grow your business, inventory these groups of activities periodically. Review the inventory and decide those which you must do, those which you can delegate and those which you can eliminate.

Develop yourself and others. Athletes who perform at any level—professional or amateur—don't stay sharp without regularly working on their skills. They understand the importance of self-development and training. The same should hold true for you.

Make your own self-development and the development of others an important part of your business from the beginning. Create a self-development plan. Read relevant books or attend training sessions, seminars, and workshops to strengthen or learn new things. Maintain an attitude for continued self-improvement and encourage that in those that you hire. As you build your organization, encourage coaching and mentoring. As you grow your business, invest in the development of the people you hire. Make self-development a part of your culture from the very beginning. Support your employees in their own personal development. Recognize the value you create by investing in the people you bring on board.

I believe that the most important assets in any business or organization are THE PEOPLE! Products don't get created or manufactured without people. Processes don't get developed or implemented without people. Customers aren't served by machines, software, and applications without people. These are all great tools. However, a tool is only as useful as the hands that design or operate it. Invest in your people. Help them understand their development needs and show them how they can improve. Challenge them to improve, to do their best. Hold them accountable. Hold yourself accountable. People, people, people are your most important asset.

Pace yourself, reward yourself. As you take on the challenge to do your own thing remember to pace yourself; don't be afraid to take a break. Time off and vacations are good. Create time for them and use them judiciously. If you work at it, you will realize that you do not need to be in touch with your business all the time. Unfortunately, many of us have become so addicted to our cellphones and electronic devices that we think they need to be by our side and activated 24-7. But we can give up these devices for a time. It is possible to sever the electronic umbilical cord to your business or organization while you take a vacation or sabbatical or just short periods of time off. You should try it.

And guess what? You will find you won't lose anything—in fact you often gain plenty as you energize, recharge and recalibrate.

Reward yourself and your team for your successes. Give yourself credit for your accomplishments. Look back on them to see what you learned and look forward to maintain your vision. Similarly, reward your team members or other individuals in your business for their own successes and their contributions to the organization. Celebrate your wins and their wins together. Make celebration a regular and acceptable part of your business culture.

Change. In Chapter Fourteen I discuss the topic of change. I encourage you to read it as you think about doing your own thing. However, I will take this opportunity to remind you to understand your behavior style and how you deal with change. If you are more of a creator than a reactor, know that your business needs to include those who can react and adapt to the change that you create. If you are more of a reactor than a creator, know that your business needs to include those who can help you identify the need to change. For more on this topic, please refer to the earlier chapter devoted to change.

Surround yourself with good advisors. Although you may be doing your own thing, you don't have to do it alone. Every successful person I have met has their own set of personal advisors to help them. As you build your business, identify advisors that can help you grow your business utilizing their area of expertise.

For example, let's assume you have been a successful salesperson in your first career. You consider yourself very knowledgeable about the sales process and how to build relationships with potential customers. Identify someone who has skills that you are lacking or that are undeveloped to be one of your advisors in the business's early stages. It could be an attorney, a banker, an accountant, a human resources expert, or just someone you admire that has demonstrated success in building his or her own business. Share your business ideas with them on a regular basis and listen to their advice. Incorporate their ideas into your plans. As the business builds success, continue to identify additional opportunities to bring in other advisors with relevant skills. Over time, you will build a solid team of advisors who may become board members if you choose to establish a more formal governance as your business grows.

Be passionate. You don't have to be an entrepreneur to do your own thing. But one value you can adopt from every entrepreneur is passion. Whatever you decide to do, if you are not passionate about it, why do it? Passion is difficult to define, but here are some examples of what I mean:

- A chef who has one of the most respected restaurants in the world and decides to close it because he has a passion to focus on culinary creativity. He turns his efforts to opening and building a foundation devoted to it.

- A successful business manager decides he wants to affect the lives of others by delivering messages of hope and caring to audiences around the world. He steps away from his "safe" business career to become a motivational speaker.

- A researcher or scientist focuses solely on determining the cause of a specific illness to develop a cure or a specific drug or other treatment to mitigate the illness.

- A youngster founds a nonprofit agency initially administered by children and committed to empowering young people to lead environmental and social change.

These are but a few examples of what I mean by "passion". I am sure you can identify many more examples of people who shape their life to achieve their dream, their passion. I challenge you to give yourself the gift of dreaming. Take some time out of the hustle and bustle of your daily life and identify your dream. What does it look like? What does it feel like? Once you have identified your dream, build your plan to achieve it. If you have a passion for something in life, but your job or career is not related to that passion, you should give some serious thought to making a change. And, what better time to begin thinking or planning it than before change is thrust upon you?

As I grew through my first career, I thoroughly enjoyed working at Arthur Andersen. I set individual goals for myself at different stages in my career and, in most cases, I achieved them. However, when I began to think about what I would do next—after I "retired," I went in a different direction. Instead of continuing to move on in the accounting and finance world, I opted to become an executive coach. A number of factors helped me move in that direction, but the primary one was the encouragement I received from some key advisors who challenged me to ask "What was it that I really wanted to do? What was I passionate about?"

After much consideration, I decided that I would focus the rest of my working life on helping others. I concluded that the best way for me to do that was to become an executive coach. Over the years, thanks to the benefits of working at a great firm like Arthur Andersen, I gained some tremendous business knowledge. I then enrolled in some formal coach training. Since then, I have combined my business knowledge and coach training to create my executive coaching practice. This second chapter of my life has been very rewarding. I keep active in business because substantially all of my clients are business people. Through other relationships I have developed, I have learned the importance of sharing my skills with other nonbusiness organizations. Coupling business knowledge with my coaching skills allows me to help others. It is my passion.

Don't misunderstand me. I had a wonderful career with Arthur Andersen in the first chapter of my business life. It taught me, expanded my horizons, helped me create lifelong relationships; it rewarded me. I would not give that up for anything. I would gladly do the same thing all over again! But, I don't need a "do-over." My first career provided me with the foundation to fulfill my passion in my second career.

Also, understand that your passion and your career do not need to be the same. I have met many people who have a passion for something other than their regular job. They love music, or woodworking, or collecting sports memorabilia, or crocheting. They do their regular jobs very well. But their career goals are secondary to the other things they love to do. Their career supports their passion.

If you are not presently engaged in your passion, I encourage you to try and get there at some point. If you haven't found your passion yet, there is time to do so. At various stages of our lives, many of us spend our time going through the motions. We take on the next job, or challenge, or career because it is there; or because we must due to our commitments or obligations. I agree that sometimes we must do so; it is our only alternative at the time. I presume that the people I referred to in the examples above lived through similar periods in their own lives. But, then something happened. They dreamed. And then they acted. Why not you?

CHAPTER 18

———

CREATIVITY

If I have not mentioned it before in this book, I enjoy the movies. I see a good number of motion pictures every year. One of the many movies I enjoyed was *Steve Jobs*. After seeing the film, I started thinking about the subject of creativity or innovation—and the occasional peril I feel when I think someone expects me to be creative—like when my editor suggested I write a chapter on this particular subject. Really? What could I possibly say about creativity?

How many times have you been asked, or told, to be innovative or more creative? How have you felt when challenged to tap into your innovative gene? Do you leap forward and accept the challenge to demonstrate your Einsteinian skills? Or do you react like Punxsutawney Phil, retreating to your anti-innovative hovel when creative expectations loom?

Creativity and innovation are a part of our everyday life, just not always in the way in which we think they are. Think about these two definitions from Merriam-Webster.com:

> **Innovation**—a new idea, device, or method; the act or process of introducing new ideas, devices or methods; the introduction of something new.[33]

> **Creativity**—the ability to make new things or think of new ideas.[34]

Throughout my career, I have had the opportunity to work with people who I believe are very creative, innovative types. Of course, I used to think that I was not one of them. I am not an innovator the likes of Leonardo da Vinci, Michelangelo, or Isaac Newton. I haven't developed new ideas like Wilbur and Orville Wright, Albert Einstein, Marion Donovan, or Dr. Temple Grandin. I haven't designed and built new products or services like Lee Iacocca, Bob Noyce, Gordon Moore, Bill Gates, Steve Jobs, or Joy Mangano (from another recent movie). When challenged to write a chapter for this book on innovation, I asked my favorite question—why me?

But as I began to assemble my thoughts on this subject, I attended two disparate events. One was a presentation on brain science; the other was an executive book presentation. In the first, I heard Dr. Sandra Bond Chapman, an eminent cognitive neuroscientist and Founder and Chief Director of the Center for BrainHealth at The University of Texas at Dallas, speak. She commented on innovation and its positive effects on brain development. Simply stated, engaging the brain in new and different activities stimulates brain health. Much like engaging latent muscles in new and different activities stimulates physical development and growth.

The second presentation was by Randy Mayeux, a consultant, educator, and trainer. He gave an executive book presentation on a book titled *Originals: How Nonconformists Move the World* authored by Adam Grant. During his presentation, Randy explained that Grant's book provides us " . . . something of a template, teaching us all how to become more of an original."

So after attending these two events, I concluded that it is healthy for my brain to practice my creative skills. I do not need to be "born an innovator"; I, too, can create. So now I challenge you to think about your creativity and how you can become a more innovative and creative person.

Somewhere in our behavioral DNA, we do have the innovative or creative gene, even those of us that may run in the opposite direction when someone mentions the word "creativity." I agree that in every person the degree of this behavioral competency is different, but I posit that it exists nonetheless. So if you, my reader, are one of the vast majority of those who deny their creative ability when challenged to use it, think of the following:

- Was there ever a time in your life when you found yourself regularly stuck in traffic and decided to try a new way to get back and forth to your office or your home—and it worked?

- When you think back over your career, did you develop a project or a process idea, no matter how great or how small, that contributed to moving an idea forward in your organization? Or, did you simply contribute your ideas to such development if you did not do it all yourself?

- If you have had the blessing of raising children, do you recall the help you have given them to solve one of their own problems—with homework, a science or technology project, or how to handle a difficult relationship with one of their classmates—even if they asked you to help them with a subject in which you did not consider yourself knowledgeable?

- When was the one time when you were in a company or department brainstorming session and you thought of connecting one idea to another that initially seemed not to be connectible at all?

- How did you feel about the situation in your past in which you were trying to solve a problem and you kept thinking and re-thinking it based on past experiences; and then all of a sudden, one of Mr. Edison's light bulbs went on and you felt or thought you found your way out of the dilemma?

I guarantee that if you take the time to formulate questions like these and think about the answers, you will remember some very successful instances of your own creativity and the very positive feelings that resulted from finding a solution. Remember, being creative is not just shaping a new idea out of nothing. It often involves applying something you have learned in your past to solving a new problem.

When we think of innovators, we think big. Big names. Big ideas. However, creating something new or different does not have to happen in big, gigantic leaps. Think of the small steps a chef takes to create a new recipe. She experiments with different combinations of flavors, spices, etc. to enhance dishes. And, generally, she only does it for a short period to add something to the menu—driven more by the desire to create than to sustain. Or what about the sales clerk that looks at every approaching customer and thinks, "How can I create a positive experience for this person?" Successful sales people are creating new ideas all the time. The act of creating something new can be a big, bold step—a series of little, baby steps—or a combination of both.

Understanding that creativity and innovation doesn't have to happen on a large scale, I started to think more about my own experiences and do you know what I realized? I do have creative talent—more than I usually give myself credit for possessing. And I am innovative. Not in the same way in which we often think of innovation and creativity, but in my own way. I have had new ideas. I have introduced new ideas to others and I have successfully sparked new ideas in others.

Looking back on my first career as an accountant and consultant, I was often challenged to come up with a new way of thinking to help a client solve a problem. As an executive coach, I have been rewarded when I ask a client a particular question and I can see the "light bulb" go on in their mind as I have provoked them to an "aha moment". By creative questioning, I am helping them deal with problems or issues they face. If you think about your own life and career, you will also reflect on numerous occasions in which your question or idea provoked change or positive action. That is you being creative.

Now that you know that there is creative DNA in your system, here are some ideas you can use to stimulate your own creativity and help others do the same with theirs. Try them on for size the next time you are challenged to be creative:

Do some self-brainstorming. One way to help manufacture new ideas or new ways of thinking is the age-old technique of brainstorming. While brainstorming may not always be the best method, it nearly always produces results. The beauty of brainstorming is you not only do it with members of your team, you can do it by yourself! Create a list of questions to stimulate your thinking. Write down three to five individual responses to each question on a single note paper or Post-it® Note.[34] Assemble all the notes on a white board or the wall and sort them by category. Stratify the various categories by degree of difficulty and flush out the workable from the unworkable. Take the results and begin your analysis of how to proceed.

Brainstorm with your team or other groups. Most of us are members of teams. While you can discipline yourself to apply brainstorming techniques in the confines of your own space, I heartily recommend doing it with your team if the nature of the issue is such that they can participate. And remember, background and skill level are not always important to the process of creating a new idea. So include any members of your team, and even some outsiders if possible.

One of my favorite and easy-to-use brainstorming techniques is called the Nominal Group Technique.[36] There are different variations of it, but the method I learned is a four-step process as follows, led by the team leader or a facilitator:

- Idea generation. Ideas are silently generated and recorded by individual participants. The facilitator asks the questions and each participant writes out their answers to each question. Each participant is encouraged to generate three to five answers to each question.

- Idea recording. The facilitator takes one answer from each participant at a time around the room. The answers are recorded on some medium—e.g., white board, flipcharts, electronic device. The facilitator continues to go around the room until each participant has exhausted all of their answers.

- Idea discussion. Once all participants have shared their answers, the facilitator leads a discussion of each idea which has been recorded. This phase is only to obtain clarification, understanding and if necessary, the logic behind an idea. The facilitator reviews the answers with participants to clarify any points so that everyone understands them. It is during this time only that other participants are given the opportunity to ask clarifying questions. If there are numerous answers and some of them seem to be similar in content, then the group should combine similar answers under one topic. There is no debating of the strength or weaknesses of any idea.

- Idea voting. A confidential vote on the ideas is then taken from the group to prioritize the ideas.

Upon completion of the meeting, someone is appointed to summarize the information for action and follow-up by the team.

The benefits of using nominal group technique are: (1) individual participation is balanced and influences of the "stronger voices" are minimized; (2) those who might not normally speak out in meetings are encouraged to participate in a positive manner; (3) more ideas, in both number and creativity, are normally produced; (4) participants generally feel that they have a greater sense of participation and accomplishment; and (5) participants generally have a better understanding of the ideas and points of view of others.

This nominal group technique is an effective, tried-and-true method to solicit innovative ideas from your team. I recommend you give it a whirl the next time you have an opportunity to do so.

Try, try again. I have often heard it said that Edison failed 10,000 times before he invented the light bulb. While I think that has been disproved as urban legend, Edison himself is quoted as saying: "I have not failed. I've just found 10,000 ways that won't work."[37] All of us should know by now that you cannot change things or create new things or solve new or old problems by doing the same thing over and over. Didn't Albert Einstein say that doing the same thing over and over again and expecting different results was the definition of insanity? So, as you apply this step, make sure that what you are trying is different from what you did the last time.

Clear the air. If you work in a place where everything is familiar to you, change your environment. This doesn't necessarily mean schlepping off to the North Woods and living in a cabin, but it does mean putting yourself in a different place for a bit of time. Once there, reflect on your issue; I'll bet this different environment helps influence your thinking. Just getting out of the normal workplace and taking a walk can often help. If you want to change your thinking, consider changing your environment.

Think differently. I attended a leadership session that had a section on creative thinking and the speaker challenged us with an idea that I have found I can use on my own to help me do this. It's a simple test. Pick out one object in the room around you. Think of how many different uses there are for that object other than its current use. Write them down. Then apply a similar thought process to the issue or problem you are trying to solve.

Draw a picture. Draw a picture of the current problem. Draw another picture that shows what things look like when the problem is solved. Despite the fact that, if like me, you are not an artist and all of your people are basic stick figures, this approach can help stimulate new thinking.

Apply different solutions to different problems. For example, did you know that Post-it® Notes were discovered by accident? According to Wikipedia, a scientist at the 3M Company accidentally created a weak adhesive that four years later a colleague of his used to invent the sticky note.[38] So, learn to look in the non-typical places to discover how certain problems can be solved. Then, challenge yourself to apply that solution to your own problem.

Analyze the data. Data mining and data analysis have become huge functions in business and organizations today, if not entire industries unto themselves. Creative problem-solving ideas can come from applying one of the earlier techniques—brainstorming—to a focused assemblage of data relating to the problem. Different people with different minds and different perspectives will observe data differently and draw different conclusions about it. Combining brainstorming techniques with data analysis can often yield new, creative results.

Use different minds. I come out of the world of finance and accounting. My college education and first career were focused on those areas of expertise. As I look back on various problem-solving sessions I participated in with other similar types throughout that part of my career, I can see similarities in the solutions that were developed. They take root in the basic background that we all had. On one occasion, my firm sent me off to a leadership seminar which included numerous other leaders from the same firm, but from different organizations and geographic areas within it. As a part of the program, we were challenged in groups of teams from different backgrounds to come up with a solution to a particular problem. I was amazed at the variety of different, creative, and innovative ideas that came from this unrelated group of my fellow partners. In my career after public accounting, I have had the opportunity to lead brainstorming sessions of people with disparate backgrounds and experiences. I continue to be fascinated by the creativity and innovation that is stimulated when a group assigned to solve a problem is cross-populated with people of varied backgrounds.

It is nearly impossible to think of where we might be without innovation or creative thinkers. Where would we be without new ideas, enhanced processes, or better products? Innovation and creativity propel us forward and prevent us from becoming stagnant. They challenge us to be more, to do more, and to create more. Yet most of us would agree that we are not working to our creative potential. But why? Why do we shy away from creativity and innovation? Are we afraid of failing, think it is too much effort, or have we indirectly been taught to stifle our creativity at times?

As I think about this, I am reminded of my two grandchildren. I love to be with them, to share in their growth and development. One thing I notice as they grow—their "natural inquisitiveness" or what might be considered some penchant for creativity, slowly diminishes over time. I think one of the reasons is that because as good parents and grandparents, we teach them the "right way" and the "wrong way" to do things. I know we do this in some instances to protect them, e.g., the "right way" to cross a street. But in some instances, are we teaching them the "right way" or "our way"? I thought about this when I was showing my grandson "how to do" a jigsaw puzzle Grampa's way. And later, after doing a few puzzles with him, I noted that he has developed his own way despite my "guidance"—and good for him!

I believe this not only occurs with children as they grow up, it also occurs in schools and in business. Have you ever heard someone say, "That's not the way we do it here? You have to do it this way. That's how we always do it." This approach can work for some organizations for a period. But any great organization recognizes the importance of "breaking the mold" occasionally. Think about it. How much do we impact our own creativity as we grow older and conform to accepted patterns of behavior? Are we limiting our ability to be creative and innovative as we learn the "correct" way of doing things?

So, if you don't think you are creative or innovative, practice some of the techniques I mentioned in this chapter. Whatever technique you devise or use, try different approaches to practice thinking differently or creatively. I am confident that you will find out that you do have creativity in you. That you are more innovative than you thought. After all, I thought I wasn't innovative or creative either. Then I wrote this book. Right?

CHAPTER 19

————

DISFLUENCIES

If I were to ask you to list a few things that you fear, what would you say? Spiders? Unemployment? Death? Flying? Heights? We all have things that make us fearful. Consequently, we all have ways in which we deal, or don't deal, with those things that arouse fear within us. Some of us avoid anything that may cause fear. We may run rapidly in the other direction to avoid these situations at all costs. Others of us may try to alleviate the fear by learning coping mechanisms to help counteract the fear.

At any point in your personal or professional life, have you been asked to speak in front of a group? Maybe you had to give a speech at a wedding, a presentation in front of the board, or train a group of new employees. How did you respond to this request? Were you nervous? Did you attempt to avoid the situation completely or try to quickly learn to cope with the nerves?

Did you know that surveys regularly cite public speaking as one of the top items people fear? Even for those who are comfortable talking in front of groups, there is an ongoing fear of using "umms," and "ahhs," and other hesitation words—or as I like to call them, disfluencies.

According to Dictionary.com, disfluencies are "impairment(s) of the ability to produce smooth, fluent speech; an interruption in the smooth flow of speech, as by a pause or the repetition of a word or syllable."[39] The use of disfluencies in your speech muddles your message and distracts the listener. They can also diminish credibility and cause your listener to doubt the message being delivered. Eliminating or even cutting down on the number of disfluencies can keep your listener more engaged and at the same time reinforce your credibility.

In researching this topic, I found an Internet article titled "How to Cut Crutch Words When Giving a Speech."[40] I found this article helpful in my own speech and have incorporated several of the ideas here in addition to thoughts from my personal experiences and those of other speakers and coaches. Think about these tips as you prepare your next presentation. You can even utilize them in your everyday conversation.

When it comes to disfluencies, awareness is a key component. Simply paying attention to how often you use them will help you make a conscious decision to reduce their frequency. You will find the following points most helpful when preparing for a formal presentation and also when dealing with disfluencies in less formal conversations.

Practice, indeed, makes perfect. It has been said that a famous musician was approached by a stranger on the streets of New York and was asked, "How do I get to Carnegie Hall?" to which he replied, "Practice, practice, practice." While this is more of an example of unclear communication messages being sent and received, I believe the musician's answer is the most important tip to help anyone remove hesitation words from their speaking habits. If you ignore every other tip I include in this chapter, be sure to implement this one. The more you practice your delivery, the more you will reduce disfluencies. Your speech should be as natural sounding as you can make it—an extension of yourself. Practice helps you achieve this level of delivery.

As part of your practice efforts, try this. Read a complex and comprehensive business article aloud before you practice your own material. (I personally favor *The Economist* as a good source). This helps you focus on the material. A better focus builds confidence and increases your ability to deliver the presentation without inappropriate or unnecessary pauses.

Another practice technique is to record your presentation, listen to it, and pay attention to the places in which you use disfluencies. Think about what might have caused the disfluency and work to remove it. With the recording devices available today, this is easy to do in the confines of a small office, conference room, or your home.

Rehearse your presentation. Every time you "umm" or "ahh," start over. If this becomes too challenging, break your presentation down into sections. Apply this technique to each section. When you successfully complete an "umm"-less section, recognize it and reward yourself.

You can also rehearse in front of an audience. Gather a few colleagues, friends, or family members to listen to your delivery and offer a critique. It doesn't matter if the rehearsal audience is familiar with your topic. You are rehearsing with them to iron out the kinks in your presentation style, not to understand the material.

Don't be afraid of over-preparation. Know your material inside out. Knowledge builds confidence. Confidence eliminates nervousness, and less nervousness results in a better presentation.

Count. As you rehearse with colleagues, friends, or relatives, ask them to observe your practice sessions and to count the amount of times you utter an "umm," "ahh," or a similar disfluency. During the delivery of your presentations, ask a colleague to count them for you. Also, ask them if they notice any sections of your presentation in which you insert more disfluencies than others. You should even ask a trusted colleague to serve as your counter during regular business meetings. The more you are aware of your own level of using disfluencies, the more you will focus on eliminating them. I appreciate that it is not always easy to receive feedback from others about our communication or delivery style, but colleagues, friends, spouses, and relatives can provide very valuable feedback if you are open to it.

Ban disfluencies from all conversations. Eliminate "umms" and "ahhs" from all conversations—even those with friends and family. The more aware you are of their existence in every conversation, the more you will build the habit to eliminate them. One technique you can employ for situations that are not public speaking involves a colleague. Discuss with him or her your desire to improve your communication skills by removing disfluencies. Ask them to listen carefully when you are making a point at a meeting, or presenting a point of view in any conversation. As before, have them count the number of times they hear you use an "umm" or an "ahh." Keep your own log of these instances and I guarantee that over time you will see a decrease in frequency, and eventually you will drive them out of your conversations.

Pauses and silence. If you feel an "umm" or "ahh" coming on, take the opportunity to pause. Also consider pausing at the end of a key point, sentence, or phrase. Make note of places in which you think a pause is appropriate; when you get to that point, pause, be silent, and count five seconds. Silence is your friend. Learn to use it. If you find yourself stuck, take a moment to pause and be quiet; you can look around the room at your audience. While you are doing this, your brain will be going a gazillion miles an hour to recover from your stuck point. Silence, truly, is golden and a second or two is not a lifetime. Once again, this is also a technique you can build into your informal presentations and everyday conversations.

Highlight. If you use a prepared speech or comprehensive notes, underline or highlight key words and phrases; or, put them in ALL CAPS. This technique helps you understand where to slow down and emphasize an individual word. When you slow down to emphasize words, this reduces the temptation to inject disfluencies.

Enthusiasm. Show an appropriate level of enthusiasm for your communication. Have sufficient confidence in your own ability to deliver a formal presentation or run a meeting. If you are enthusiastic and show some emotion in your presentation, it is easier to avoid the use of "umms" and "ahhs."

Work extra hard on the hard stuff. Every presentation has a beginning, middle, and end—even informal ones. Make sure you practice your introductions and final thoughts or conclusions sufficiently so that you can repeat them consistently. If there are complex sections of your presentation, first try to reduce the complexity to help your audience understand. But if complexity must be delivered, practice it until you can do so effortlessly.

Plan and organize your notes. Use a comfortable medium for your notes—prepared outline, note cards, copies of PowerPoint slides, iPad, etc. Organize them in a fashion that allows you to feel comfortable in your delivery, but also provides you with the appropriate anchors if you get stuck.

Focus on quality. If you have to provide large volumes of information, consider supplementing your speech with detailed notes or slides for the audience to take with them. Your presentation should be about quality, not quantity. Some of the best speakers posit that a great presentation makes no more than three major points. Don't try to take fifteen minutes of material and expand it to an hour-long presentation. Doing so almost guarantees you will fill your presentation with "umms" and "ahhs."

Don't apologize. If you do make a mistake in your presentation, or you use an inadvertent "umm" or "ahh," don't stop and apologize. This can distract your audience's train of thought and, worst case, throw you off yours.

Seek reduction, not elimination. Focus on reducing the number of disfluencies you use. When you have reached substantial improvement, most others will think you have eliminated them altogether. If you strive for total elimination, you might lose focus on your delivery, and this can botch up your presentation.

Look for outside help. Consider joining Toastmasters®, or a similar organization.[40] Toastmasters® is one of the best organizations to help improve speaking skills. They have chapters all over the world. In fact, in some large organizations, internal Toastmasters® programs are offered. These programs help improve speaking style in all areas, not just disfluencies. They also help with the finer points of presenting—such as gestures, tone of voice, body language, and content. By working on these skills, you will have the confidence you need to speak in front of any audience.

By eliminating "disfluencies" or "crutch words" from your speech, you will not only deliver more powerful presentations, you will enhance your daily communications. You will present better at company meetings; if you are in sales, you will be more confident in front of potential customers; if you are in transition, you will be more confident when meeting with recruiters and interviewers.

Disfluencies do not have to be a way of life. If they are an issue for you, you can deal with them by following any of the simple steps I have outlined in this chapter. Reducing disfluencies in your speech will build your confidence and help ensure your message is heard. You will also increase your credibility among your audience because um, they won't, a-h-h-h be distracted by those u-m-m-m, gap fillers, right?

CHAPTER 20

―――

WORK/LIFE BALANCE

A few years ago, my wife and I returned from a terrific trip we had with some friends through various parts of France. In all, we spent three weeks on two cruises in addition to some land exploration. Upon returning home, I reconnected with a number of people, some of whom were clients at that time and knew I had been on vacation. I couldn't believe the reaction that many people had to my time away from work. Comments from my friends and colleagues ranged from, "I could never take that much time away from work," to "I don't know how I could possibly be away from my job for that long," or "I can't wait until I am retired so I can take a trip like that."

I acknowledge that I am not working full time. I also admit that when I was working full time, I never took a vacation that long probably due to the same reasons my colleagues had the reaction they did. Now that I am older, and hopefully, somewhat wiser, I find myself wondering, "Why not?"

As I have just spent some time writing about doing your own thing, transitioning and networking, it only seems appropriate to discuss how to find a balance with so much going on. Work/life balance, or as one of my clients once put it "Work/life imbalance," is a topic that frequently comes up in my coaching and mentoring work. It is often on the minds of many of us that juggle both a family and a career. What is work/life balance, and how do we achieve it?

First and foremost, it is important to understand that you are in control of your work/life balance. Not your boss, your spouse, or your kids—just you. Very often, we want to blame others for the imbalance that exists in our own lives. We want to point the finger at others for over-scheduling or over-demanding. However, it is up to you to find and maintain a balance in your life that works for you. One that allows you to feel balanced in both your personal and professional lives.

If you want to achieve some definable work/life state, you must define what it means to you, assess your current situation, develop a plan to achieve it and work your plan to reach your goal. No one will do it for you. No one else will make this happen. Believe it or not, you are in control. So, get started by asking yourself the following questions:

- What does work/life balance mean to me (and to those important to me)?

- How is my work/life balance currently?

- In what areas do I feel that I need to improve my balance?

- What can I do to help create balance in my life?

- What are the barriers I face to achieve work/life balance?

- What types of support do I need from family and colleagues to help me improve my work/life balance?

- What does satisfactory work/life balance look like to me, and how will I know I am achieving it?

As you answer these questions, you will more specifically clarify what is not in balance. Once you understand what is causing you to be out of balance, you can begin to make the necessary changes to improve your work/life balance.

I have worked with two different senior executives in two different companies whose jobs were in one city and whose families and homes were in another. Both of them regularly commuted back and forth between their company's locations and home. Both of them had good personal lives and met or exceeded their work responsibilities on a consistent basis. They were very successful in their respective roles. They had determined what was a good balance and were in control of maintaining it. When each of them accepted their positions, they had separate conversations with their family members about the impact on their family lives of being separated during the week. They also had specific conversations with their new bosses and their direct reports to explain how they were going to manage their responsibilities. They made it clear to their employees that they did not expect any of them to change their work habits because their bosses would be putting in long hours during the week so that they could fly home to visit their families on weekends.

In another situation, I worked with a manager who complained that her boss had different expectations with respect to the hours she should be in the office. Consequently, this created difficulties with her personal life. She had a situation at home with an elderly relative that required a certain amount of attention and care; she was frustrated because she "had to be in the office early every morning and stay after normal business hours." When I inquired why she "had to do this," she told me it was because of her boss. "He is always here and he expects me to be here as well." She was encouraged by her mentor to have a crucial conversation with her boss about this particular "requirement." Over time, with compromise by both, it was resolved to her satisfaction. And, as a part of the better communication that developed between her and her boss, she learned that it was never an expectation of her boss that she spend so much time on site. However, his behaviors were driving her to the conclusion that she should be physically present much more than he expected.

In the first example, the executives could easily have had significant imbalance issues upon taking their new long-distance position, but they each developed plans for dealing with the issues of living and working from different locations. This allowed them to help establish a good balance in their lives.

In the second example, a balance problem was brought under control by establishing good communication between the person affected and her boss. Unfortunately, it is easy to make poor assumptions about what is expected both at home and at work. We change our behavior based on what we think others expect of us before we know what they actually expect from us. So, before you make any drastic changes to create balance, it is beneficial to fully analyze the situation—think straight—and communicate your plan to resolve it—talk straight. Figure out why imbalance exists and then devise a plan to correct it.

There are many reasons why imbalance can happen.

Failure to properly delegate. Do you believe that those working for you can handle additional responsibilities? If so, are you challenging them properly? Or do you believe it is "more efficient" for you to perform certain work or tasks yourself? As a leader, if you don't have the right people to whom you can delegate responsibilities, then you don't have the right people. One of your leadership responsibilities is to develop the people that work for you. Develop your successors. If they cannot meet your expectations, then you must deal with it—train them, reorganize or restructure them, or replace them. Having the wrong people in positions will result in more work for you and create imbalance in your life.

Insufficient numbers. Do you have enough people to whom you can delegate tasks? If you don't have enough people to do all the tasks, you either have to obtain more people, reduce the number of tasks that have to be performed, or increase the productivity of the team.

Culture. Is the culture of the organization such that everyone has to "put in the hours" as an expectation of good performance? If that seems to be the case, I would first look around and see if everyone is "putting in the hours." If other successful members of the organization seem to have found a way to avoid the hour crunch, learn from them. If it truly is the culture of the organization, evaluate what that means for you as an individual and take appropriate action. Only you can decide if the culture of the organization is one that allows you to create a work/life balance.

Boss's expectations. In this case, it is not the culture of the organization. Instead, it is that people believe their boss expects them to "be here all the time" or "be available 24-7". If this is your lot, it merits a conversation with the boss. Is this an incorrect assumption or a clear expectation? Once you have had that conversation and clearly understand his/her expectations, you can plan your life and act accordingly.

After you gather the facts and understand why imbalance exists, build your plan to create better balance. Maybe you can even begin to plan your own three-week vacation.

To get started, recognize that you will need to make changes. Like with so many other things you want to change, your first step is to develop a plan. In other chapters, I have talked about planning in greater detail. You can refer to those discussions, but some simple thoughts to consider are:

- Gather your facts. Define what this work/life conundrum means for you. As you do so, focus on the future. What is your vision? What is important to you in your life, in your work? What will a better-balanced life look like for you? Consider your beliefs, family, friends, church, community, society, politics, personal well-being (spiritual, mental, physical), career progression, the nature of the work you would like to do, etc.

- Identify barriers. What are some of the barriers you face to improve your balance? Who or what can help you overcome those barriers?

- Measure progress. Set a time frame to measure your progress, assess where you are, identify the gaps, and plan executable steps to close the gaps. As you set goals, remember the Management 101 acronym—SMART. Goals should be Specific, Measurable, Achievable, Realistic, and Time-framed.

- Involve others. As necessary, and once you are ready, discuss your plans with those close to you. Start in the home and within your circle of friends. Incorporate their input into your plan. Ask them regularly how you are doing and allow them to hold you accountable for your committed, actionable steps.

- Implement your plan. Take your plan into the workplace. Understand your organization's policies and modify your plan accordingly. Discuss them with your mentor or coach, your human resources support, your boss, and your team. Respect and appreciate their concerns. Be flexible and compromise, but do not compromise beyond your acceptable limits.

As you attempt to find a better balance within your own life, it is essential to recognize that change will need to occur. It is also very common to slip or regress at certain times as demands change. However, by implementing some of the following tips, you can help maintain a focus on your work/life balance plans:

- Take your spouse on a date, your child to work, or a family member on a business trip.

- Schedule "take-it-home" work around your family activities and responsibilities.

- Turn your phone/PDA/laptop off at certain times; use technology to enable, not disable.

- Encourage employees and teams to deal with issues together; don't try to solve all their problems yourself.

- Set up a personal "Run with your son" or "Hit the water with your daughter" commitment on a scheduled basis.

- Outsource certain chores.

- Schedule "down time" for yourself.

I believe that if you have an issue with "balance," it can be worked out with communication and appropriate planning. However, no one can plan or communicate it but you. As you embark on this balance journey, here are some additional tips to consider:

- Know your behavior style. I have said this before, and I will say it again. Your behavior style affects everything you do—how you think, how you communicate, how you learn, and how you grow and develop. Know your style and understand how it affects your approach to this issue.

- There are only 24 hours in every day. You get the same total as everyone else—no more, no less. Use your time wisely.

- Ed's Add and Subtract Rule. As you add items to your life and work "plates," you have to subtract others. When you take on additional roles and responsibilities, you grow and develop. When you delegate roles and responsibilities to others, you help them grow and develop.

- Sharpen your time management skills. If your abilities to organize your life are hindered by poor skills in this area, you will not succeed.

- No matter what you think, you can't do it all, you can't have it all, and you are not entitled to it all.

- Seek out other resources. There are some very good books that you can use to help you with this process. One of my favorites is *Off Balance: Getting Beyond the Work-Life Balance Myth to Personal and Professional Satisfaction*[42] by Matthew Kelly.

- Economic times today are more difficult than they have been in my lifetime and, I trust, in yours. Workplace uncertainties are more common than ever. Yet these are not reasons to avoid dealing with your own work/life balance issues. In fact, they are all the more reasons why you should find proper balance. There is no better time to start than the present. Begin to develop your plan. You cannot control everything, so control what you can.

- Recognize the effect of stress on your life, and redouble your efforts to care for yourself—exercise, take stress breaks, meditate, read, listen to your favorite music, etc. Incorporate these healthy behaviors into your plan as well.

Often, when I am working with individuals on finding work/life balance I hear, "These ideas won't work around here." My response is simply this: If your plans won't work "here," you may have to define a new "there." Very often when our life is out of balance we forget to take care of ourselves. As you strive to find and maintain a good balance it is important to remember who comes first in your life. You do. Don't forget your need to grow and develop—physically, mentally, and spiritually. You can best take care of others or fulfill your myriad of responsibilities if you first take care of yourself. Finding your balance is one of the steps in doing that.

Many years ago, I heard this quote and I think it is relevant to our topic here. Brian Dyson, CEO of Coca Cola Enterprises from 1959 to 1994, is quoted as saying, "Imagine life as a game in which you are juggling five balls in the air. You name them—work, family, health, friends and spirit. And you're keeping all of these in the air. You'll soon understand that work is a rubber ball. If you drop it, it will bounce back. But the other four balls—family, health, friends, and spirit are made of glass. If you drop one of these, they will be irrevocably scuffed, marked, nicked, damaged, or even shattered. They will never be the same. You must understand that and strive for balance in your life."[43]

I believe that you can have "balance" in your own personal and professional life—but only if you define what that means for yourself and build your own plan to achieve it. Once you establish a good work/life balance, you will be so surprised that you were ever out of balance. You may even schedule your own three-week vacation!

CHAPTER 21

GRATITUDE

As I have mentioned, the process of writing this book was long. At times, it was difficult, intense, and time consuming. Personally, I am proud of myself for my commitment to and completion of a project that was not easy to do. More importantly, I am thankful to you, my reader, for taking the time to read what I have to say. I appreciate the fact that you chose my book. Thank you.

Over the last several years, I have begun to realize that gratitude is something rarely expressed. For some, we may not even think about thanking someone for something they did. For others, we may think about thanking someone but fail to put our thought into action. Think for a moment about your own life. When was the last time you thanked someone? The last time you expressed your gratitude to someone else? Has it been a day? A week? A month?

One of my favorite stories about gratitude is the Charlie Plumb story. He is a former Navy fighter pilot and prisoner of war (Vietnam). I have heard several versions, but here is the story from Captain Plumb's book, *I'm No Hero*.[44]

As told by Capt. Plumb:
"Recently, I was sitting in a restaurant in Kansas City. A man about two tables away kept looking at me. I didn't recognize him. A few minutes into our meal he stood up and walked over to my table, looked down at me, pointed his finger in my face and said, "You're Captain Plumb."

I looked up and I said, "Yes sir, I'm Captain Plumb."

He said, "You flew jet fighters in Vietnam. You were on the aircraft carrier Kitty Hawk. You were shot down. You parachuted into enemy hands and spent six years as a prisoner of war."

I said, "How in the world did you know all that?"

He replied, "Because, I packed your parachute."

I was speechless. I staggered to my feet and held out a very grateful hand of thanks. This guy came up with just the proper words. He grabbed my hand, he pumped my arm and said, "I guess it worked."

"Yes sir, indeed it did," I said, "and I must tell you I've said a lot of prayers of thanks for your nimble fingers, but I never thought I'd have the opportunity to express my gratitude in person."

He said, "Were all the panels there?"

"Well sir, I must shoot straight with you," I said, "of the eighteen panels that were supposed to be in that parachute, I had fifteen good ones. Three were torn, but it wasn't your fault, it was mine. I jumped out of that jet fighter at a high rate of speed, close to the ground. That's what tore the panels in the chute. It wasn't the way you packed it."

"Let me ask you a question," I said, "do you keep track of all the parachutes you pack?"

"No" he responded, "it's enough gratification for me just to know that I've served."

I didn't get much sleep that night. I kept thinking about that man. I kept wondering what he might have looked like in a Navy uniform – a Dixie cup hat, a bib in the back and bell bottom trousers. I wondered how many times I might have passed him on board the Kitty Hawk. I wondered how many times I might have seen him and not even said "good morning," "how are you," or anything because, you see, I was a fighter pilot and he was just a sailor. How many hours did he spend on that long wooden table in the bowels of that ship weaving the shrouds and folding the silks of those chutes? I could have cared less...until one day my parachute came along and he packed it for me."

When I read this story, I think, who are the special people in my life who provide the encouragement I need when the chips are down? Perhaps its time right now that I give those people a call and thank them for packing my chute.

Throughout our careers, we have read leadership books, attended behavioral workshops, been professionally mentored or coached, or been involved in group discussions about how to work or relate with each other in a more effective way. We have learned about how we can behave more positively, work more productively, communicate more effectively, build better relationships, and be a better leader. In many of these books, seminars, webinars, and conferences, we have often heard about treating others with respect, following the golden rule, or adopting an "attitude of gratitude." We have participated in conferences, held one-on-one discussions, sat through "wisdom circles," listened to motivational CDs, and learned other techniques to help us do so. Then we left the seminar, turned off the webinar, or put down the book and went back to our regular behavior. Our behaviors did not change based on our new knowledge. But why?

For many of us, change is difficult. Changing behavior is even more challenging. Often, we don't change our behaviors because we think we don't have the time. In reality we are just too distracted with other thoughts or commitments to challenge ourself to change our behavior or do something different from what we ordinarily do. We simply don't take the time to make change happen.

So, I ask you again. When was the last time you thanked someone? The last time you expressed gratitude to someone else? After all, how difficult is it to thank:

- The members of your team when they meet a milestone on a project?

- Your direct reports for showing up on time for a meeting?

- Your teenage son or daughter for their academic, sporting, or artistic success in school?

- Your spouse for remembering a family member's birthday?

- Your mail carrier, newspaper delivery person, lawn maintenance crew, or your house cleaning personnel for their regular, dependable service?

- A colleague for a networking introduction?

- Your parents for being good parents or your children for being good children?

- Your boss for her mentoring, guidance, or help on a project?

- The barista for preparing your coffee order properly?

I could go on and on with this list, but the point is that I believe we have let gratitude slip out of our lives. Our lack of gratitude hasn't been due to any dramatic shift in our culture, it has been a slow drip-drip-drip of lost courtesy. So, I challenge you to make gratitude a part of your everyday life. For example, the next time you interact with the clerk in your local convenience store, greet them with a smile and thank them for helping you. If someone in your office has just made a mistake, thank them for their efforts and help them understand how to move forward in a positive way. If someone in your family has just done something that you think is "stupid," rein in your emotions, take a deep breath and explain your difference of opinion about their action in a rational, thoughtful manner. Then, thank them for being who they are and tell them what they mean to you.

In addition to each of us taking small moments out of our lives to express our gratitude to others, we could also do a better job of accepting gratitude when it is given to us. In most cases, it is sufficient to respond to a gratuitous comment with a simple, "You're welcome." But in some instances, we might want to expand on our recognition of the appreciation given to us. I had a client a number of years ago who was working on this very behavior—showing her gratitude to others in various situations. She had come into a company in which the culture expected this type of behavior. But she had come from an organization which was lacking any kind of gratitude principle. In one particular situation, she expressed her thanks to one of her direct reports for completing a project before the stated deadline. Her direct report said back to her, "I appreciate you taking the time to thank me for this work effort. You know, as I have gotten to know you over the past six months since you joined our company, I was not sure that I was living up to your expectations. This is the first time I remember you thanking me for the work I did, and I appreciate it very much." There is no rule for how two parties should express gratitude and gratitude recognition to each other, but I think all of us could do it more often.

Another aspect of gratitude I recommend you consider is called "pay it forward." It simply means that you honor a good deed that someone did on your behalf by performing a simple act of kindness for someone else. There have been books written on the idea; numerous famous persons have quoted some form of pay-it-forward as being important in their lives; there is even a not-for-profit Pay It Forward Foundation.

We may not all be "do-gooders", but we can strive to be "do-betters". As we pay it forward and do better we will ultimately start to feel better, too. When we feel better, we do better and our actions may even ignite positive behaviors in others.

There is a theory related to human behavior that I have heard. It takes twenty-one days to create a new habit. I have tried it and been successful with it and I feel confident that it will work for you too. So, I challenge you to express more gratitude in your life. Start tomorrow morning. Before you hustle off to the bustle of the workday, or tomorrow evening before you lay down to rest, make a list of three to five people you will interact with the next day. Think about how these people affect your life in a positive way. The next time you interact with them, remember to thank them for the interaction. At the end of the day, review your list and assess how you did. Then make your list for the next day. Try this for three weeks, consecutively, or twenty-one days and see if it becomes a habit.

The Charlie Plumb story at the opening of this chapter says it all. Gratitude is a powerful force. Use it appropriately and you will feel its power. Thank those who pack your parachute.

What better way to demonstrate that we care than by expressing our gratitude? So again, thank you for reading my book. Thank you to the person that encouraged you to read this book. And thank you to all the individuals in my life that influenced me and encouraged me to write this book. I appreciate you.

CHAPTER 22

―――

STORIES

The first eleven years of my professional career were spent working in Chicago. Chicago made sense since I had lived my entire life in the Windy City. In the start of my twelfth year with Arthur Andersen, I was asked to transfer to Dallas, Texas. My exposure to Texas at that point had been through stories about Roy Rogers, Gene Autry, Hopalong Cassidy, Matt Dillon, Paladin, the Alamo and, of course, J.R. Ewing. I was up for the challenge and accepted the transfer.

Shortly after I began working in the Dallas office, one of my senior partners asked me to accompany him to visit a small, potential client in East Texas. On the three-hour drive, he explained that he wanted to introduce me to this client because I had significant experience working with clients in this particular industry. But he reminded me several times that my background was significantly different than the CEO's and cautioned me that I might not feel as if I were "fit" to serve this company.

The CEO was not in when we arrived, but his secretary escorted us to his office to wait for him. I had not been in an office like this before. The walls had their share of mounted animals and fish, hunting and fishing paraphernalia, and weaponry. Pictures of the CEO in outdoor gear with a number of local, state, and national celebrities also adorned the walls. The CEO gregariously entered the office in a western shirt, jeans, and cowboy boots. I immediately felt a bit unnerved in my three-piece suit. As the meeting began, my partner and the CEO engaged in running commentary about the hunting and fishing season and some of the adventures they both had participating in these activities. I could not and did not add much to that part of the conversation. At the appropriate time, my partner opened the conversation about me serving the company. He explained my background and understanding of the industry. At this point, I joined the conversation and expressed my interest in learning more about the company. While I spoke, the CEO kept quiet, listened, and nodded at some of my comments. I explained my background, the reason the firm had transferred me to Dallas, and my interest in serving his company. He listened diligently and when my partner finally asked the CEO if it would be a good fit to have me on the job, he replied, "Well, y'all are clearly a Yankee, but as long as you know your stuff and you don't show up at every meeting with a lawyer by your side, we should be able to work together." And do you know what? We did. We worked well together for several years.

This experience from years ago is a story I have told and retold in many different situations to make a point. This story is a part of who I am. It is one of the many stories that I use to help teach others or convey a point. Stories, when used correctly, can aid in comprehension, help build relationships, and create interest.

Mankind has been using the power of storytelling for thousands of years. Did you know that one of the oldest recorded stories in history dates back 11,000 years? We see evidence of historical storytelling in archaeological digs and cave wall carvings. Storytelling has been part of our DNA throughout history and is still actively used today. Businesses, organizations, and families use stories to pass along culture, traditions, history, and values. We tell stories to help our children learn, to explain our beliefs, and to describe the places we live. We tell stories to emphasize a point, to describe a process, to build relationships. We use stories to make points about any subject, anytime and anywhere.

How we tell a story is nearly as important as the content of the story itself. Think about some of the stories you have heard. When was the last time you heard a good story? I mean a really good story! You know, the kind that you can remember every last detail. The type of story you want to tell over and over again. Now think about some of your more recent conversations. If you were able to recount every conversation you had in a day, how many stories would you have shared with others? How many stories would you have listened to during every day conversation?

Naturally, most of my stories relate to my personal experiences and most of your stories result from your own experiences. I have many stories from my career at Arthur Andersen, from my career as an executive coach, from my volunteer work in the community. I have stories from my personal life, from my own successes and my own failures. I have even accumulated some good stories from listening to others. My stories include diverse topics such as great client service and poor client service, personal successes and personal failures, business development highs and business development lows, performance evaluations that went very well and performance evaluations that did not go so well, communication highlights, and communication gaffes. It even occurred to me that I sometimes tell a story without realizing I am telling a story. In fact, I will also wager that as you read the first sentence of this paragraph, your mind brought back some stories about some of your own experiences. That's the power of storytelling!

Stories, when told well, engage people on many different levels. Since many stories are told in order to trigger action, we must connect on an emotional level in order to effectively use the power of storytelling. Consider the following:

- When was the last time you convinced someone on your team, or your entire team for that matter, to take action without telling them some sort of story to motivate them?

- How often have you used a personal story or a story about someone else to teach people how something works?

- When have you, or someone on your team, explained how another group inside or outside your company achieved success in creating a new product or service or coming up with a new product or service idea?

- Have you used a personal event in your own past to demonstrate a strength or weakness to others?

These are but a few of the reasons we tell stories. Other examples can be found in Stephen Denning's *The Leader's Guide to Storytelling/ Mastering the Art and Discipline of Business Narrative*.[45] His book is a great reference about the types of stories you tell and how to tell them. In it, Mr. Denning gives some great examples of stories for each of eight different narrative patterns he describes. The primary narrative styles we use to tell stories in business, according to Mr. Denning, are to spark action, to communicate who you or the company/firm are, to transmit values, to foster collaboration, to tame the grapevine, to share knowledge, and to lead people into the future. I witnessed the power of storytelling at a business reunion where I was able to reconnect with friends and colleagues not seen for many years. Upon entering the event hall, I was immediately met with familiar faces from the past. Several of the people who greeted me at the registration table were people who had done so at different events throughout the years. This brief interaction immediately brought back memories of similar events. As I walked around the room, I had the chance to visit with many people from the past.

Some people recounted serious issues from our past work together, calling to mind difficult situations and how we resolved them. Others saw nothing but humor in the past, and recounted situations that brought laughter to everyone's lips. Some people told stories of colleagues who were no longer with us, but helped us recall fond memories of our time together. Others brought up stories about similar events in the past and how we benefited from coming together periodically as a group. Some of the attendees brought along mementos of past work and experiences, further jogging people's memories to tell stories about colleagues and events from the past. Much of the evening was spent telling stories about events in our past.

In all, it was a great evening and revitalized some of the camaraderie we had as members of the same organization. Since the event took place, I have participated in numerous conversations with people who attended, as well as those who did not attend. Recounting the event with them was just another story I was able to share!

So, while stories may sometimes be a part of everyday conversation, should you attempt to plan stories for particular conversations? Of course, but that depends on the nature of the conversation, its degree of importance, and what your goal of the conversation is. If you are trying to convince someone else to purchase your product or services, you might want to relate a story that reflects how the service or product has benefited a customer in the past. If you are delivering a performance evaluation, you might want to tell a story about how an evaluation affected you in the past. The nature of the conversation and the degree of the point you are trying to make will help you assess how much planning you put into the stories you tell. The significance of the points you are planning to make in the conversation will affect the degree to which you need to plan the stories you tell. Just remember that if you begin to tell a story that comes to mind "out of the blue," give yourself a few seconds to sort out the beginning, middle, and end so the story is delivered well and the points are clear to your listener.

Stories have been with us since the beginning of time. They are serious. They are funny. They are fact-based. They are opinion-based. They make you angry. They make you sad. They make you happy. They help us learn. The best ones always make a point.

Recognize the benefit of good stories. Use them effectively to help engage your listener and make your point. Think straight to organize them. Talk straight to tell them.

CHAPTER 23

———

STEWARDSHIP

Noise. Words. Social media. TV. Music. iPods. iPads. Tablets. Face-to-face communication. Phone conversation. Texting.

With the amount of information we are presented with every day, it is a wonder we don't spend our entire life in a state of over stimulation. But occasionally, there is a single thought or concept that breaks through the noise and resonates with us. This single concept can have such an impact on us that we remember it for a long time, even years later.

Many years ago, during my fresh-out-of-college job interview with Arthur Andersen, a very senior partner introduced me to the concept of stewardship. It was a new concept to me, and one that I really had never given much thought to. At the time, I, like many other people, associated volunteerism with stewardship. It wasn't until this interview that I understood stewardship happens in all types of organizations.

The definition of stewardship provided during that interview many years ago has stuck with me throughout my entire career. He said, "Stewardship means it is my responsibility to make this a better place for the people that follow me because those ahead of me made it a great place for me."

Being young, fresh out of college, and a bit more egocentric, I was not thinking about stewardship and how my actions would affect those that follow me. But over time, the concept of stewardship really resonated with me and I find myself sharing it often with others as I move through life.

Ideally, everyone would act like a steward regardless of their title within an organization. However, this is not always the case. Most, if not all, of you who read this book are leaders at some level in your organization. Whether you are leading a project team, a department, a division, or a company—you are a leader. As a leader, you should accept your responsibility not just to lead but to act as a steward as well.

So how do leaders who are stewards behave in their role? I believe:

- They first and foremost care about their people.

- They create an environment in which everyone works together towards a common goal.

- They build trust with their team.

- They act with integrity at all times and expect nothing less of their team.

- They have the competence to do their job and the knowledge that goes with the territory.

- They set the vision and define the mission; they inspire their people to achieve them.

- They understand the organization's culture; they believe in it and live it every day. They walk the talk.

- They provide others—colleagues, direct reports, teammates, etc. with the tools they need to get the job done.

- They take responsibility for their actions and expect others to do the same.

- They hold their team accountable, fairly and equally, to achieve their tasks.

- They stand out of the way and let their team perform.

- They reward them, individually and collectively, when they have accomplished their tasks.

- They change course when the environment dictates the need for change.

- They communicate the results of the team's attempts, achievements, and failures.

- They listen to feedback and act on it.

- They communicate, communicate, and communicate again.

- They mentor, develop, teach, and coach others.

- They control that which they can, and they do not worry about that which they cannot. If it is something they cannot control, they take responsibility to deal with it accordingly.

- They act responsibly to protect the environment and build the community.

- They take care of their physical well-being and that of their team.

- They seek to learn and develop.

- They think straight. They talk straight.

- They know to have fun, and they do.

- They know to rest, and they do.

Ironically, most of these characteristics are the same characteristics that define a good leader. In fact, you will notice that my lists for stewardship and leadership overlap. That's because good leaders are stewards, and stewards are good leaders.

If you do these things, I believe you will leave behind an organization, a community, a society and an environment that is better than it was when you got there. You will be a good steward.

In business, most of my examples of effective stewardship come from observing many of my fellow partners at Arthur Andersen. Over the years, I was regularly impressed at the efforts they put forth to make our firm a better place. Did they have a profit motive? Absolutely! You can't provide stewardship in any business if you aren't growing it responsibly. For example, I watched partners make sacrifices to invest in the education and professional development of our people by acquiring a small private college and converting it into a model professional education and development facility. Other partners sacrificed when they moved into a fledging business called "administrative services," which eventually grew into one of the largest consulting firms in the world. Still other partners in the 50s and 60s made personal sacrifices to move to foreign countries to help build our own international network. They created professional service firms in those countries that had the same culture and attitude towards service as the organization in the United States.

There are many other good examples of stewardship in business. Any organization whose core value is to grow a better place for its people and all of its other stakeholders is an organization of good stewardship. These organizations promote an attitude of caring, giving back, and growing the business in a responsible manner. Many also refer to this as servant leadership.

Beyond business, you will find good stewards in your community. Here are a couple of examples that come to mind for me:

- A few years ago, a friend of mine identified a need related to the local education system. She saw a need for teachers who aspired to be principals and administrators to have a more formal development program. Working with others in the community, she developed a plan, assembled the appropriate resources, obtained all necessary approvals, and started an organization that prepares educators to become principals and lead change within their own schools and school districts. She is a great example of a steward for our community. Her actions created a better system for those that follow her.

- Two other local leaders I know identified a need to bring consistency and quality to organizations which offer after school programs for children. Working together and building on their own community relationships, they founded a successful organization which helps other organizations achieve nationally-recognized quality standards in their after-school programs.

What examples of stewardship have you seen in your business, community or personal life? What have you done to be a good steward?

Those who are stewards accept the personal responsibility to help plan for the future. Unfortunately, many of us are so wrapped up in the present that we forget that our actions and decisions of today affect the generations that follow us. We are so focused on the present that we don't think about the future. And often times, we are so focused on ourselves that we forget about others.

Sometimes individuals recognize the need for stewardship, but don't want to put forth the effort, or don't think they know how to do so. Truth be told, stewardship requires effort. Often times, a lot of effort. This is one reason why many individuals are not stewards. They view it as somebody else's job. However, good stewards are able to see the positive impact that their actions will have, and are willing to put forth the effort to make the future a better place. If you believe that building stewardship in your organization is important, you must make the effort to contribute to that value. Otherwise, why are you there?

Don't let your focus or passion for your own goals stand in the way of being a good steward and be willing to put forth the effort. If you want to be a steward, concentrate on how you can make your little piece of the business or the organization a better place for those around you. You own the space around you—your "personal space." If you have some supervisory, managerial, or leadership responsibilities in your organization, you also own the space in that part of the organization. Start thinking and doing what you can to improve that space for everyone in it.

It is possible for everyone to be a good steward. By becoming a good steward, you can promote stewardship within your organization and leave it better than when you started. Start small. A few small changes can create a big impact. So ask yourself, what can I do tomorrow to make my organization a better place? Do this daily and you will find that not only will you become a better leader, but a model steward as well.

CHAPTER 24

────

LEGACY

Throughout my career, many individuals encouraged me to write my ideas down in a book. As I stated in the Introduction, I would give it a quick thought and then move on to the next activity at the time. It wasn't until I began to write this book that I began to think of my legacy and how this book could play a role in my life both now and in the future.

Have you thought about your own legacy? Have you thought about what it will be? What would you like it to be? I believe it is something we should give thought to, and in this chapter I hope to stimulate your thinking about your own legacy and how you have the power to create your own.

Throughout the time I have been writing this book, experiences with friends and family have reminded me of the frailty of life. As I have entered the later chapters of my life, these reminders come with more frequency than the wedding and birth announcements of my younger years. For some, this may be a morbid thought or a depressing subject. But whether you like to think about it or not, I believe your legacy is worthy of your time and personal reflection.

As you move through the different stages of your life, have you thought about what you will leave behind? Of course, there are plenty of sources around to help you decide what to do with your properties, your life insurance proceeds, your assets, your collections of dolls or baseball cards. That is why we have investment advisors, wealth planners, attorneys, and accountants. Tangibles aside, what about you? What is the essence of you that you will leave behind?

When I ask around, I sense that legacy is a subject most people don't think about very often or at least not until "later in life." If you ask someone what their legacy will be, they usually have a quick, sarcastic answer. They may even avoid the question by deflecting it altogether. Or they might immediately switch to a discussion of the aforementioned doll or baseball card collection and not make a single reference to the non-tangibles they will leave behind.

I agree that the topic of one's legacy is often an uncomfortable subject for most people. But uncomfortability is not a reason to ignore the matter entirely. Many researchers have documented the fact that people who are in their later stages of life, often make contemplative comments like:

- I wish I had spent more time with my family, my kids, my friends, my spouse, or my . . .

- I wish I had the chance to give back to my community or to the XYZ charity or the ABC social entity.

- I spent all of my life building my business; I wish I knew more about the arts.

- I wish I had traveled more, seen more, or experienced more.

In various seminars, workshops, and leadership presentations I have attended, I have heard a comment like this: People on their deathbed never say, "I wish I spent more time in the office."

In other chapters of this book, I have discussed the importance of planning—your career, your life, your next project or presentation, your transition. Your legacy is no different. It also requires planning. Take the time to think about your legacy and begin to do something about deciding what you want it to be. Then work toward building it and documenting it for those who follow you.

Famous people, even infamous ones, don't have to spend much time thinking about their legacy if they don't want to. Society will create their legacy for them; although many who are smart about it will do what they can to shape theirs. Most of us don't have biographers waiting in the wings to document our lives and legacies. So, it's up to us. After all, your legacy is yours. It does not need to be created or shaped by others. Like so many other ideas I have shared with you in the preceding chapters, you are in control of your life; you are responsible for how you live. The legacy you leave behind should be shaped by you. And, here is what I suggest you do.

As you work on your own personal development plan, business plan, or life plan—whatever you use to help you focus on your objectives— incorporate some thoughts about how you want to be remembered. One easy exercise is to consider this scenario: You are an observer at your funeral. Your relatives and friends are discussing your life. What are they saying about you? What do you want them to remember you for? If you have had the blessing of children, grandchildren, nieces and nephews in your life, ask what you want them to know about you? What do you want your relatives and colleagues to remember you for? Is it the same? Are there differences?

Once you have created a list of the memories you want to leave behind, audit your list. Talk to a spouse or close relative or friend and validate that the list makes sense and is complete. After all, these are the people that know you best. They can provide some great insights and can validate your thinking. And, as is often the case, they may see something in you that you are unable to see in yourself.

Now that you have your list, compare it to your life to date and the future plan that you have for yourself. Are the lists consistent? Are you living a life that is consistent with the legacy you want to leave behind? If there is consistency, you are on a good path. Continue to follow it. If you lack consistency, you have some course correction to make.

Once you have an idea of what you want your legacy to be, you need to set some actions to help ensure you are living a life that is consistent with that idea. For example, create three, no more than five, questions that you ask yourself once a day related to the life you are living and whether it is consistent with the legacy you wish to have.

Then, create your own scheme for monitoring your progress. Find tools that are available for documentation and choose the one that you prefer. The easier the documentation method, the more likely you are to document.

Here is a simple example of what I mean: Steven decides he wants to be remembered for providing for the future security of his family. He wants to be remembered for sharing his personal resources within his community. He wants to be remembered as someone who enhanced the lives of the individuals around him. So he creates a series of questions, such as the following:

- What did I do today to build the security of my family's future?

- How did I share my personal resources in my community today?

- What did I do today to enhance the lives of the individuals around me?

- Do I intend to do something tomorrow that will help me respond to one or all of these questions positively?

Once a day, Steven asks and answers these questions. It is best if he can designate the same time of day to do it—e.g., in the morning before breakfast, in the evening before he tucks himself in for the night, after dinner before he turns on the TV, picks up his current book, or opens some of his "homework."

If once a day is too much for you, consider a less intense schedule, but find what works for you. The point is to do it. To think about it and make it a part of your life now.

As you develop this habit, should you write these things down? Like many things, my answer is: "It depends." Are you the type of person who can keep a journal regularly? Are you the type of person who has never kept a journal, but thinks it is a good idea to try? Are you the type of person who doesn't like journaling at all and does not have the discipline to do it? Whether you write your thoughts down, record them, or even video them, you should have some type of documentation of what you want your legacy to be. Chances are, the act of documenting will increase your accountability which will in turn will increase your frequency. For additional thoughts, Google "Plan your Legacy" and you will find plenty of material to help you. Also, there are numerous individual consultants and businesses that can help you document your legacy.

To help you get started, here is a quick summary of how I have started my documentation:

- A number of years ago, a family friend suggested an interview be recorded of my parents. They used a questionnaire designed to elicit a personal family history. They videotaped my mom and dad to record the responses. At the time it was done, I thought I already knew a good bit about my parents' past. I did; but I learned some new things, too. Consequently, I have a recording going forward that I can share with our son and grandchildren that helps ensure their legacy continues to be shared.

- I took another step when our first grandchild was born. Every year on his birthday, I write him a letter. Similarly, I have begun doing so with our second grandchild. The letters are sealed and their parents keep them safe. They will be given to my grandchildren when they are old enough to read, understand, and contemplate them. It is my way of leaving something behind for them that provides them some family history and some insight into who I am.

- I began to document my own legacy when I decided to write this book. It will be another source for those in succession of my life and will hopefully give them a better understanding of who I am.

These methods are easy for me to execute, which is why they work for me. Consistent with many other things I have suggested in this book, if you like the idea, use it. If this style is not for you, then don't use it. But, do something. Design your own method to identify your legacy, live it, and pass it on to those important to you. Don't allow one of your last thoughts to be, "I wish . . . "

As I completed this chapter, and ultimately this book, I found myself in self-reflection. How would I answer the question: "What would you like your legacy to be, Ed?" As I pondered the answer to this question, I was reminded of a poem I came across while writing this book. Although I am not one for poetry, this poem resonated with me and has helped me determine my own legacy.

The House by the Side of the Road
(by Sam Walter Foss)

There are hermit souls that live withdrawn
In the peace of their self-content;
There are souls, like stars, that swell apart,
In a fellowless firmament;
There are pioneer souls that blaze their paths
Where highways never ran;

But let me live by the side of the road
And be a friend to man.

Let me live in a house by the side of the road,
Where the race of men go by—
The men who are good and the men who are bad,
As good and as bad as I.
I would not sit in the scorner's seat,
Or hurl the cynic's ban;
Let me live in a house by the side of the road
And be a friend to man.

I see from my house by the side of the road,
By the side of the highway of life,
The men who press with the ardor of hope,
The men who are faint with the strife.
But I turn not away from their smiles nor their tears—
Both parts of an infinite plan;
Let me live in my house by the side of the road
And be a friend to man.

Let me live in my house by the side of the road
Where the race of men go by—
They are good, they are bad, they are weak,
They are strong.
Wise, foolish—so am I.
Then why should I sit in the scorner's seat
Or hurl the cynic's ban?—
Let me live in my house by the side of the road
And be a friend to man.

Deciding your own legacy is not an easy task. However, for me, this poem sums it up very well. I would like to be remembered as a friend to anyone I have served in any of the roles I have had throughout my life—husband, father, grandfather, friend, colleague, coach, mentor, businessman, volunteer. If I have been a friend to others, then in some way I have helped others and this is what I want my legacy to be. I encourage you to determine your own legacy and live your life accordingly.

Conclusion

Many years ago, when learning how to do some classroom teaching and make presentations, I was told the following: Any time you present something to a group:

1. Tell them what you are going to tell them;

2. Tell them; and,

3. Tell them what you told them.

This is #3.

As stated in the Introduction, the purpose of this book is to share some of my thoughts and observations about different facets of business and organizational life that I have learned throughout my career. I also wanted to share them in a fashion that models the theme of the opening chapter—Think Straight. Talk Straight. I took up my "pen" primarily for the benefit of my grandchildren. When they are old enough, I hope they read this. It is part of my legacy, and therefore I hope it helps them understand some things about their grandfather and my outlook on business and life.

And, if you have taken the time to read some or all of this book, I thank you. I hope you have benefited from the experience.

Ed Maier, 2019

ADDITIONAL READING

Throughout the years, I have read many books which have helped form my thinking. I referenced some of these throughout my book and think they might be of interest to you. Here is a list for your consideration.

Bacon, Terry. *Adaptive Coaching*

Blumberg, John G. *Good to the Core: Building Value with Values*

Collins, James. *Good to Great, Built to Last* (with Jerry Porras)

Covey, Stephen R. *The 7 Habits of Highly Effective People*

Denning, Stephen. *The Leader's Guide to Storytelling: Mastering the Art and Discipline of Business Narrative*

Isaacson, Walter. *Steve Jobs*

Ferazzi, Keith and Tahl Raz. *Never Eat Alone: And Other Secrets to Success, One Relationship at a Time*

Frankl, Viktor. *Man's Search for Meaning*

Goldsmith, Marshall. *What Got You Here Won't Get You There*

Goleman, Daniel. *Emotional Intelligence*

Goodwin, Doris Kearns. *Team of Rivals: The Political Genius of Abraham Lincoln*

Grant, Adam. *Originals: How Non-Conformists Move the World*

Johnson, Spencer. *Who Moved My Cheese?*

Kelly, Matthew. *Off Balance: Getting Beyond the Work-Life Balance Myth to Personal and Professional Satisfaction*

Lencioni, Patrick. *Death by Meeting* and *The Five Dysfunctions of a Team*

Levinson, Daniel J. *The Seasons of a Man's Life* (with Charlotte M. Darrow, Edward B. Klein)

Lucht, John. *Rites of Passage at $100,000 to $1 Million+: Your Insider's Lifetime Guide to Executive Job-changing and Faster Career Progress in the 21st Century*

Manchester, William. *The Last Lion: Winston Spencer Churchill* (three volumes)

Maxwell, John. *Winning with People/Discover the People Principles That Work for You Every Time*

Peters, Tom. *In Search of Excellence/Lessons from America's Best-Run Companies*

ENDNOTES

1. Walter H. Andersen, *Arthur Andersen: The First Fifty Years, 1913-1963* (Chicago: Arthur Andersen & Company, 1964).
2. Wikipedia contributors, "Gunning fog index," Wikipedia, The Free Encyclopedia, accessed August 16, 2017, https://en.wikipedia.org/wiki/Gunning_fog_index.
3. Stephen R. Covey, *The 7 Habits of Highly Effective People*, (Free Press, 1989).
4. IUPUI content managers, "Learning Styles," Indiana University-Purdue University Indianapolis, accessed October 4, 2017, https://blc.iupui.edu/success-coaching/academic-success-strategies/learning-syles/index.html.
5. Wikipedia contributors, "Coach (sport)," Wikipedia, The Free Encyclopedia, accessed January 1, 2017, https://en.wikipedia.org/wiki/Coach_(sport).
6. Dave Day, *Professionals, Amateurs and Performance: Sports Coaching in England*, 1789-1914, (Peter Lang AG, 2012).
7. Wikipedia contributors, "Mentorship," Wikipedia, The Free Encyclopedia, accessed January 1, 2017, https://en.wikipedia.org/wiki/Mentorship.
8. John Maxwell, Winning with People, (HarperCollins Publishing, 2007).
9. Stephen R. Covey, *The 7 Habits of Highly Effective People*, (Free Press, 1989).
10. Rich Karlgaard, "Peter Drucker On Leadership," Forbes, last modified November 19, 2004, http://www.forbes.com/2004/11/19/cz_rk_1119drucker.html.
11. Wikipedia contributors, "5 Whys," Wikipedia, The Free Encyclopedia, accessed January 3, 2017 Wikipedia, https://en.wikipedia.org/wiki/5_Whys.
12. Taiichi Ohno, *Toyota Production System: Beyond Large-Scale Production*, (Productivity Press, 1988).
13. COSO, "The Committee of Sponsoring Organizations of the Treadway Commission—White Paper—Internal Control—Integrated Framework, May 1994," accessed October 4, 2017, http://www.academia.edu/12912529/INTERNAL_CONTROL_INTEGRATED_FRAMEWORK_Committee_of_Sponsoring_Organizations_of_the_Treadway_Commission.
14. Marshall Goldsmith, "Try Feedforward Instead of Feedback," accessed October 29, 2015, http://www.marshallgoldsmith.com/articles/try-feedforward-instead-feedback.

15. Smith, Andy. *What is Appreciative Inquiry?* CoachingLeaders, LTD, 2012.
16. "Emotion." Dictionary.com. Accessed January 26, 2018. http://www.dictionary.com/browse/emotion?s=t.
17. Daniel Goleman, *Emotional Intelligence*, (Random House Publishing, 2012).
18. *EQ Workshop, Lore International Institute.* 2005. PowerPoint presentation on understanding your emotional intelligence.
19. "Attitude." Merriam-Webster. Accessed January 26, 2018. https://www.merriam-webster.com/dictionary/attitude.
20. Stacey A. Thompson and Native American Folklore, "Two Wolves," accessed September 7, 2017, http://www.virtuesforlife.com/two-wolves.
21. Luke, disciple of Jesus Christ, "Luke 6:31", BibleGateway, accessed October 4, 2017, https://www.biblegateway.com/passage/?-search=luke+6%3A31&version=NIV.
22. "Ethics." Dictionary.com. Accessed January 26, 2018. http://www.dictionary.com/browse/ethics?s=t.
23. John Donne, *No Man Is an Island*, (Souvenir Press, 1988).
24. Merriam-Webster editors, "Networking," Merriam-Webster.com, accessed September 8, 2017, https://www.merriam-webster.com/dictionary/networking.
25. Allwords editors, "Networking," Allwords.com, accessed September 8, 2017. https://www.allwords.com/word-networking.
26. Dictionary editors, "Networking," Dictionary.com, accessed September 8, 2017, http://www.dictionary.com/browse/networking.
27. "DiSC" is a registered trademark of Inscape Publishing, Inc. 6465 Wayzata Blvd., Suite 800, Minneapolis MN 55426.
28. Wikipedia contributors, "Kübler-Ross model," Wikipedia, The Free Encyclopedia, accessed June 17, 2017, https://en.wikipedia.org/wiki/K%C3%BCbler-Ross_model.
29. Wikiquote contributors, "Louis Pasteur," Wikiquote, accessed January 2, 2017, https://en.wikiquote.org/w/index.php?title=Louis_Pasteur&oldid=2185082.
30. "Inconvenient." Dictionary.com. Accessed January 26, 2018. http://www.dictionary.com/browse/inconvenient?s=t.
31. "Truth." Dictionary.com. Accessed March 10, 2018. http://www.dictionary.com/browse/truth?s=t.
32. John G. Blumberg, *Good to the Core—Building Values with Values*, (Simple Truths, 2009).
33. "Innovation." Merriam-Webster. Accessed January 26, 2018. https://www.merriam-webster.com/dictionary/innovation.

34. "Creativity." Merriam-Webster. Accessed January 26, 2018. https://www.merriam-webster.com/dictionary/creativity.

35. "Post-it" is a registered trademark of 3M Company 220-9E-01 3M Center, 2501 Hudson Road St. Paul MINNESOTA 55144.

36. Wikipedia contributors, "Nominal group technique," Wikipedia, The Free Encyclopedia, accessed September 15, 2016, https://en.wikipedia.org/wiki/Nominal_group_technique.

37. BrainyQuote contributors, "Thomas A. Edison," BrainyQuote, accessed September 9, 2017, https://www.brainyquote.com/quotes/quotes/t/thomasaed132683.html.

38. Wikipedia contributors, "Post-it note," Wikipedia, The Free Encyclopedia, accessed December 24, 2016, https://en.wikipedia.org/wiki/Post-it_note.

39. "Disfluency." Dictionary.com. Accessed January 26, 2018. http://www.dictionary.com/browse/disfluency?s=t.

40. Scott H. Young, "How to Cut Crutch Words When Giving a Speech," Lifehack, accessed September 9, 2017, http://www.lifehack.org/articles/lifehack/how-to-cut-crutch-words-when-giving-a-speech.html.

41. "Toastmasters" is a registered trademark of Toastmasters International Corporation California 23182/ Arroyo Vista Rancho Santa Margarita California 92690.

42. Matthew Kelly, *Off Balance: Getting Beyond the Work-Life Balance Myth to Personal and Professional Satisfaction*, (Avery, 2011).

43. Brian Dyson, "Imagine Life as a Game in Which You are Juggling," Goodreads, accessed September 9, 2017, http://www.goodreads.com/quotes/92129-imagine-life-as-a-game-in-which-you-are-juggling.

44. Captain J. Charles Plumb, *I'm No Hero: A POW Story*, (Self-published by author, 1973).

45. Stephen Denning, *The Leader's Guide to Storytelling/Mastering the Art and Discipline of Business Narrative*, (Jossey-Bass, John Wiley & Sons, Inc., 2005).

About The Author

 Ed Maier is an executive coach, mentor, speaker, and meeting facilitator with nearly fifty years' experience in the business field. Along with his wife Carol, Ed owns and operates a privately-held executive coaching and consulting company specializing in one-on-one coaching with managers and executives in order to advance their skills. Previously, Ed had a successful career serving as a senior partner with Arthur Andersen, a global professional services firm. He served clients, trained and developed professionals, and led a regional practice of over 1400 people. Ed is a motivational speaker with a true passion to help others, especially in one-on-one coaching situations. He is an active writer, having published over thirty newsletter articles on relevant topics within his field. He and his wife Carol reside in Frisco, Texas. To learn more about Think Straight. Talk Straight. or to request more of Ed's published work, please visit his website at www.thinkstraighttalkstraight.com or write him at ed@thinkstraighttalkstraight.com.